AN INTRODUCT

ESOL TEACHING

Jane Jordan

Acknowledgements

I am grateful to Christina Healy of Blackburn College for her valued contribution to the development of the materials in the book.

Much of the content of the book has grown out of my work at the Stockport ESOL Unit teaching students and training volunteer tutors. I am, therefore, grateful to the students and colleagues who have made this possible. In particular I should like to thank Carole Crompton, the ESOL Unit Co-ordinator, who suggested my name to ALBSU in the first place, for her valuable support and comments, and to Hilary Montrose and Rizwana Choudry for their comments and contributions.

In addition I have gained inspiration and knowledge from many of the resources listed at the end of each chapter, too numerous to mention individually.

ISBN 1 8 70741 48 X

Design: Studio 21

First edition published September 1992

Contents

Preface

This is an introduction to the teaching of English to Speakers of Other Languages. It is for anyone who intends to teach or is teaching English to adults whose mother tongue is not English. It is for volunteer tutors, teachers and trainers who have no specialist qualification in ESOL and who may work in a range of settings: adult education centres, further education colleges, open learning centres, the home, community organisations, prisons, industry, vocational training schemes.

It is intended to support people who are working towards the City and Guilds Initial Certificate in Teaching Basic Skills (ESOL 9284). This certificate is designed to enable participants to demonstrate competence in teaching ESOL to individual students. For this reason this book concentrates on the skills necessary in a one-to-one situation. It does not deal with general teaching skills such as classroom management. However, most of the content of the book will also be useful for ESOL group teachers who have no specialist training.

It is hoped that the methods and approaches described in the book reflect current practice in ESOL and that the book will provide a good grounding in the skills required to teach ESOL.

Introduction

What is ESOL?

English for Speakers of Other Languages (ESOL) provision is for adults whose mother tongue is not English and who have settled in Britain on a permanent basis. It aims to enable people to participate fully in British society and to gain access to opportunities such as employment, education and training.

A brief history of ESOL

ESOL provision was developed initially to meet the needs of immigrants mainly from the New Commonwealth countries and Pakistan who came to Britain in the late 1950s. This provision was seen as short term and was largely funded by the Home Office, the Department responsible for immigration, through Section 11 of the Local Government Act of 1966. The main providers of ESOL tuition were Local Education Authorities.

These early schemes concentrated on teaching 'Survival English', mainly to women, often in their own homes, using volunteers and some part-time teachers. A further development took place in the 1970s when Industrial Language Programmes were set up to teach English in the work-place, mainly to men.

Since then ESOL provision has developed to differing extents depending on the settlement patterns of immigrants and other local factors. There is now more group teaching, open learning opportunities and in some areas language support for people on other courses. English language help for technical and vocational purposes is also available as part of government programmes.

The need for ESOL

ALBSU commissioned a survey in Spring 1989 which was carried out in inner city and surburban areas and covered over 50 mother tongues. This estimated that, while nearly 500,000 adults needed help with English, only about 44,000 were in provision.

Of the adults interviewed 53% wanted help to improve their English, 23% were receiving help and 59% were not aware that such help existed. 30% said they had real difficulty in understanding and speaking English and 40% in reading and writing English. People not only wanted help on arrival in Britain but at key points in their lives, such as gaining employment, improving promotion prospects, helping with their child's education.

Who are the potential students?

Adults who want to learn or improve their English are not a homogeneous group.

- They have come to the UK to live on a permanent basis for a variety of reasons: to join their family, to get married, to find employment, as refugees, for business.
- They can range in age from 16 to 60 plus.
- They can have widely differing educational backgrounds: some have no formal education and are not literate in any language, some are graduates from overseas.
- They vary in their level of English from beginner to advanced and may have different levels of competence in their language skills; for example, advanced spoken skills but weak written skills.
- They come from a wide range of countries, not only the New Commonwealth, e.g. Vietnam, Iran, Iraq, Somalia, Thailand, Turkey, Spain, South American countries. Many have a non-European mother tongue with a different script.
- They may have work and family commitments which prevent them attending regularly or for more than a few hours a week.

Where does ESOL provision take place?

ESOL tuition is provided in a wide range of venues: adult education centres, community centres, further education colleges, Employment Training schemes, in the home, in prisons.

Provision ranges from direct language teaching to language support for vocational courses, in groups or one-to-one. Groups are often made up of students at different levels (multi-level) and with different first languages (multi-lingual). In some areas there may be classes which share a single mother-tongue (mono-lingual).

How does ESOL differ from EFL?

English as a Foreign Language (EFL) in the UK is aimed at people who come on a short term basis with the main purpose of learning English because of its use as an international language. They plan to return to their own country to use their improved English language skills. They tend to be young and single and to want to learn intensively by attending full-time courses. Some who are working or here with their families, e.g. 'au pairs' or business people and their spouses require part-time courses.

Classes are usually multi-lingual and are organised at different levels. They often work towards specific examinations. Provision takes place in further education colleges, adult centres and private language schools.

1 Adults as Learners

In the introduction some factors about ESOL were described which make it clear that there is no such thing as a typical student. When adults come to learn or improve their English they usually have specific present needs and future plans. They can also bring with them a range of skills and knowledge which can help their learning. Sometimes they may lack skills or have commitments which can hinder learning.

ESOL aims to meet the needs of individual students so, whether you are teaching on a one-to-one basis or in a group it is important for you to work with the student to identify the factors necessary to accommodate the requirements of the student and help learning.

Below are the profiles of five students who are in ESOL provision.

1. Sakeena

'I want to talk to the doctor and my children's teachers and I want to learn to read and write.'

Sakeena came from Pakistan twelve years ago. She did not go to school and is not literate in Urdu. She has got five children, four are at school and one at home. She used to have a home tutor but gave up because she was too busy with the children. Now she feels she has a bit more time and wants to have more English lessons. She doesn't meet many people outside her community. She can understand quite a lot of English but only speaks a little. She knows the alphabet and can write her name.

2. Thach

'I want to go on a training scheme to be a car mechanic but I shall need help with my English.'

Thach is 35 and from Vietnam. He came to Britain as a refugee with his wife and young family. He was educated to primary level and had worked as a driver in Vietnam. He knew no English on arrival but attended a short intensive course at the reception centre in Norwich.

Now, several years later he understands well and can cope with most everyday situations. His pronunciation is not very clear so sometimes people do not understand him. He can read and write English at an elementary level. Thach has passed his driving test. He worked at a car upholstery factory for two years before being made redundant.

3. Yasmin

'I am a trained teacher but I can't teach in Britain without requalifying. This will take a long time so I am thinking of training for something else. First of all I want to improve my conversational English.'

Yasmin arrived from India a month ago. She is in her twenties. Her mother tongue is Gujerati and she has a degree in history and a teaching qualification from Baroda University, in Gujerat. She has a good formal knowledge of English but lacks confidence in her ability to understand different accents and speak English to people in England. Although she would like to pursue her career as a teacher her qualifications are not recognised in this country. She is daunted at the prospect of requalifying so has decided to enrol on a nursery nursing course at a further education college as a mature student. Her previous qualifications are acceptable for entry. She can also get ESOL support while studying. While waiting to start she is attending an advanced ESOL group to practise her spoken English.

4. Omer

'I am a journalist but it will be a long time before my English is good enough to work here as a journalist. I also need to get any job to live.'

Omer is from Turkish Kurdistan. He came to Britain in 1989 as a refugee. He has settled in Hackney and is working as a presser in a clothing factory in Bethnal Green, where all his fellow workers are Turkish.

Omer was a journalist in Turkey and was persecuted for his beliefs. He speaks Kurdish and Turkish. He learnt French at Secondary School and completed University education in Istanbul. Most of his family are still in Kurdistan and he is deeply worried about them.

His original intention was to learn English as quickly as possible and take up his journalistic career again but found it necessary to take any work he could. He attends an Open Learning Centre to learn English. He is very tired when he arrives for lessons and his progress in English is disappointingly slow.

5. Ladda

'It was very difficult when I first came because I could not understand much English and I couldn't read or write at all. Now I know quite a lot but I want to learn more so I can get a better job.'

Ladda came to Britain from Thailand in 1990 with her English fiance. She spoke practically no English. She had attended primary school and is therefore literate in Thai. She worked as a cleaner and in a restaurant. She is now married and obviously gets plenty of practice listening to and speaking English at home. She is very determined to acquire good English language skills. She has attended a beginners

ESOL class and has now come to an ESOL workshop where she can work with a tutor on her individual needs. She works part-time as a school cleaner and in a Thai restaurant at the weekends.

What do these profiles say about the needs and aspirations of these students?

Sakeena needs to improve her use of English in everyday situations such as health and shopping. She needs to build on her understanding and develop her confidence in speaking. She wants to be able to communicate with teachers herself rather than be dependent on her husband. Being able to read and write English is an important step to being more independent.

Thach needs the English to deal with job search and interviews and to cope with a specialist training course. He will also have to deal with official letters and communicate with his children's school. A particular language need will be to improve his pronunciation.

Yasmin first needs to practise listening to a variety of accents and speaking in everyday contexts. When she starts her course she will need to concentrate on English for study purposes.

Omer's aim is to get a job commensurate with his experience and training. He would need fluent and accurate English for this. He needs to think whether this is realistic in the short term. In the meantime training for alternative employment with language support may be possible. English for interviews and job search is an immediate need.

Ladda needs English for everyday purposes; shopping, health, travel, and for social conversation with her husband and his family and people at work. She also needs specific work related English and job search and interview skills.

What skills do the students already have?

Sakeena has a considerable passive knowledge of English to build on. She is good at running a home and family. She is an excellent cook and very good at sewing and embroidery.

Thach is literate in his first language and in English and has acquired quite good spoken skills in English. He has work experience as a driver and in a factory, relevant to his preferred occupation.

Yasmin has high academic qualifications and therefore has study skills in her first language. She has a good formal knowledge of English.

Omer is also well educated in his first language and has learnt two other languages so will feel competent to learn English to an advanced level. He has the skills required for journalism in Kurdish and Turkish.

Ladda has basic skills in her first language and has work experience as a cleaner and restaurant worker which she is already putting to good use in Britain.

What barriers do the students face and how can they be overcome?

Sakeena's lack of education in Pakistan makes learning difficult for her. She has no transferable skills. The demands of her family means that she does not have much time for study. She does not want to go out to a class while she still has a young child at home. She lacks confidence in her English, especially as her husband and older children speak English quite well. She feels embarrassed to speak in front of them in case they laugh at her. She doesn't get much chance to practise with anyone else. A home tutor is the first step to overcoming some of these barriers. She can choose a convenient time to have her lessons and build up her confidence in using English.

Thach lacks formal qualifications and the confidence in English to take up a training course. His pronunciation difficulties give the impression to employers that his English is weaker than it is. He has to support his family so financially he could not attend a course unless paid while doing it. The government funded course he has been offered is ideal for him especially as he will get language tuition at the same time.

Yasmin's formal experience of learning English means that she lacks confidence in using everyday spoken English. This can easily be overcome by giving her plenty of practice in an advanced level class. The fact that she cannot transfer her qualifications is harder to deal with. She could decide it was worth spending the time to requalify or, as she has decided, to find a suitable alternative which will not take so long and which will take some of her prior learning into account.

While **Omer** has got excellent transferable skills the level of English required to be a journalist in Britain is daunting. Financially he is unable to attend full-time English classes. He is often too tired to study and he has no-one to practise with. His concern for his family makes it difficult for him to concentrate at times. He could look for alternative employment in which he would be with English speaking people and which might leave him less tired or aim towards a government funded course. He could continue his open learning lessons, learning new skills and have more opportunities to use his English.

Ladda is fortunate in that she has few barriers to learning. She has no formal qualifications and has had to learn a different writing system. Her work commitments

12

restrict the times and the number of hours she can attend classes. However, her work experience is more important that qualifications in getting a job and eventually she may be able to attend a training course to upgrade her skills. As she works in the afternoons she is able to attend four hours of English a week in the mornings.

Such an analysis can be shown on a chart like the one below.

Name: **Sakeena**		
Needs and Aspirations	*Language Skills*	*Other Skills*
• English for health, shopping, talking to teachers • Basic literacy	• Fluent Punjabi • Quite good understanding of English • Some speaking skills	• Organising • Parenting • Cooking • Sewing
Barriers to learning	*Ways of overcoming barriers*	*What else?*
• Family commitments • Lack of previous learning skills • Lack of confidence • Few opportunities to practise	• Home tutor • Community group with creche • Encouragement	• Local mother and toddler group • Joining in parent-teacher activities

Further reading

A Nation's Neglect: Research into the need for English amongst speakers of other languages, ALBSU 1989.

There are a number of books and readers which give cultural background and describe the personal experiences of people who have come to live in Britain. For example:

Asian Women Speak Out: a reader, Amrit Wilson and Julia Naish, National Extension College, 1979.

A Language in Common, Marion Molteno, Women's Press, 1987.

Our Lives: a series of readers, Croydon Language Scheme Book Group, 1990.

2 | Planning a Learning Programme – 1

ESOL is about trying to meet the needs of individual students. In order to do this and to plan an appropriate programme, whether the student is to be taught individually or in a group, the processes of assessment and negotiation are essential. Initial assessment is about finding out what the student already knows and what needs to be taught. Negotiation is essential because you and the student will have your own ideas about what should go into the learning programme. It is important that you are both involved in this planning procedure and that the outcomes are agreed by both of you.

What are the processes involved in establishing learning priorities?

1. *Finding out* as much as possible about a student: previous learning and experience, present circumstances, long and short term goals, perceived needs.

2. *Analysing* the goals in order to identify the language elements and levels of competence needed to achieve them.

3. *Assessing* a student's current competence in the four language skills (listening, speaking, reading and writing).

4. *Negotiating and planning* a programme of work, setting short term objectives for a specified timescale.

These processes do not necessarily take place in a fixed order and often overlap. Your initial assessment may have to be modified as you find out more about the student's competence.

The diagram on page 15 shows the procedure described and also introduces the concept of ongoing assessment and evaluation which will be dealt with in more detail in Chapter 9.

How can these processes be carried out?

1. Finding out about a student

Informal interview

When a student first comes to seek provision s/he will usually have an informal interview with a tutor or organiser. Most of the necessary background information can be acquired at this interview and recorded on the form used by your ESOL programme. As this may be the student's first contact with the programme it is important that the interview is private, friendly and non-threatening.

If a student is not a complete beginner the interview may be conducted in English. This has the advantage that the interview can also become part of the assessment of the student's level of competence in spoken English.

If a student is a beginner the interview should be conducted in the mother tongue, either directly by a bi-lingual tutor, or through an interpreter. It is preferable to use an objective interpreter but this is not always possible and students often bring along a friend or relative to interpret for them. The use of an interpreter with students who have limited skills in English can ensure an accurate exchange of information, avoid misunderstandings and enable a student to express desires and hopes with ease. It can also emphasise the abilities and skills of a student rather than her/his limitations and it is invaluable when negotiating a learning programme as this can involve difficult vocabulary and abstract concepts.

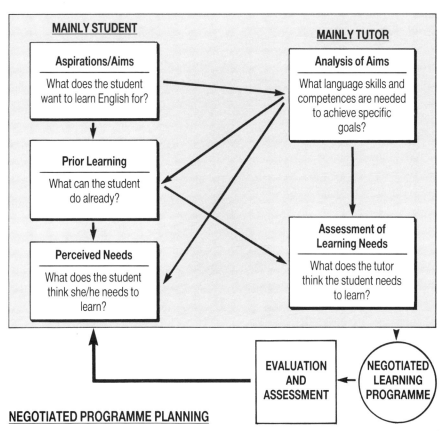

NEGOTIATED PROGRAMME PLANNING

15

PLANNING A PROGRAMME   Date ....

Student's name ....   Tutor's Name ....

What do you want to use your English for:

	Tick box		
1. With neighbours, friends, colleagues	☐	7. TV and radio	☐
2. In shops, banks, post office	☐	8. With my children's teachers/To help my children with their education	☐
3. At the doctor's, dentist's, clinic	☐	9. To read newspapers, books, magazines	☐
4. With officials: at door, Town Hall, by post, (letters, bills, forms)	☐	10. To help me get a job	☐
		11. To help me in my job	☐
5. For travel: bus, train, car, plane	☐	12. To help me get a place at college or on a training scheme	☐
6. Using the telephone	☐	13. To help me in my studies	☐

**Checklist A.
Urdu**

ابتدائی تعین   پڑتال کی فہرست ۔ اے

تاریخ

طالبِ علم کا نام

آپ اپنی انگریزی کس مقصد کیلیے استعمال کرنا چاہتے ہیں

نشان لگائیں

١.   ہمسایوں ۔ دوستوں اور اہل کاروں کے ساتھ

٢.   دوکانوں ۔ بینک اور ڈاک خانے میں

٣.   ڈاکٹر اور ڈینٹسٹ کے ساتھ اور کلینک میں

٤.   سرکاری علاقہ کے ساتھ ۔ ٹاؤن ہال میں ۔ خط و کتابت ۔ بل اور نام پڑ کرنے میں

٥.   سفر کیلیے ۔ بس ۔ ریل گاڑی ۔ کار اور جہاز میں

٦.   فون پر بات کرنے میں

٧.   ٹی وی اور ریڈیو کے لیے

٨.   بچوں کے استادوں کے ساتھ اور بچوں کی تعلیم میں مدد کرنے کیلیے

٩.   اخبار ۔ کتابیں اور رسالے پڑھنے کیلیے

١٠.   نوکری حاصل کرنے کیلیے

١١.   نوکری میں مدد کیلیے

١٢.   کالج میں ٹریننگ کیلیے جگہ حاصل کرنے کیلیے

١٣.   میری پڑھائی میں مدد کیلیے

*Rizwana Choudry:
Stockport
ESOL Unit*

16

PLANNING A PROGRAMME

Break down the goals into smaller parts.
This checklist will help you identify the elements.

Listening
- Identify people's feelings, attitudes
- Understand telephone messages
- Understand the main points of a conversation, talk, lecture, news item
- Understand the details of a talk, conversation, etc.
- Understand questions
- Understand instructions
- Understand explanations
- Understand British accents

Speaking
- Give personal information
- Greet people and make social conversation
- Ask and answer questions
- Describe people, things, events
- Tell people what happened
- Talk about experiences
- Talk to people on the telephone
- Pass on a message
- Leave messages on an answerphone
- Ask when I don't understand
- Ask for or offer help
- Explain a problem, give reasons
- Give instructions
- Take part in a discussion
- Say what I think or feel
- Agree or disagree
- Express apologies, thanks, sympathy
- Invite people, accept and refuse invitations
- Tell people my future plans
- Read a story aloud

Reading
- Read signs and notices
- Read forms
- Read timetables, maps, diagrams
- Read messages
- Know alphabetical order
- Use a dictionary
- Use a telephone directory
- Understand newspaper headlines
- Understand the main points in an article or story
- Identify the important information in advertisement
- Understand abbreviations
- Understand instructions
- Read reports
- Understand formal, official language in letters and bills

Writing
- Fill in forms, timesheets
- Write cheques
- Write short messages
- Write a formal letter
- Write about my experiences and interests
- Write instructions
- Make notes when listening to someone
- Make notes about something I have read
- Write reports
- Write essays
- Write a list of information about myself for job applications (curriculum vitae)

Name: Sakeena		
Goal: To practise the English needed when going to the doctor		
Skills and Knowledge	Can Do	Needs To Do
Listening: To receptionist offering appointment times To instructions, explanations or advice from doctor **Speaking:** Making/Changing an appointment Reporting to receptionist Greeting Describing symptoms Giving details of the history of illness/problem Asking for information/explanation Asking the chemist for medicine **Reading:** Details on an appointment card Name of medicine and instructions **Writing:** Signing prescription form		

Name: Thach		
Goal: To learn and practise the English needed to be a car mechanic		
Skills and Knowledge	Can Do	Needs To Do
Specialist vocabulary. **Listening:** To instructions To explanation of a problem **Speaking:** Asking questions to clarify the problem/job Explaining what the problem is Saying what you have/haven't done Asking for help Asking where things are Ordering parts Using an appropriate style when speaking to workmates, supervisors, customers **Reading:** Instructions A manual Understanding a diagram Service checklist **Writing:** List of parts used Ordering parts Description of job completed Timesheet		

Checklists

These are useful as a guide to you and a student in selecting long-term goals and short-term objectives. Some examples of checklists are given on pages 16-17. Checklist A, for example, can help a student to identify the general areas s/he wants to work on. Such a checklist is not necessary for a student whose main goal is clear from the outset, such as **Thach** who needs language to help him with a training course and **Yasmin** who needs support for her studies.

Checklists can be in English and/or the mother tongue and can be used for self assessment of prior learning as well as identification of needs.

2. Analysing the goals

Breaking down the goals

A long-term goal is usually very broad and achieving it may seem daunting. Therefore it needs to be broken down into the skills and knowledge needed to achieve the goal. This may help a student to realise that s/he knows some things already and to clarify what still needs to be learnt.

Checklist B may help you do this breakdown. Some of the items can be subdivided even more into small manageable objectives. This kind of checklist requires considerable analysis and uses abstract concepts. The use of the mother tongue is an asset with students up to intermediate level. At this stage it may be preferable for you to select the skills needed for the student's goal and then discuss them with the student giving examples like this:

Skill	Usage in health context	Example
Give description	Describe symptoms	*I've got a headache and I feel sick.*

If you are supporting a student on a training scheme or a college course you will need to consult the tutor on the course content and the communication skills needed in order to make an analysis.

On page 18 are some examples of analysing a goal.

Levels of competence

A checklist does not show the level of competence in a particular skill. You need to consider what level is required to carry out a task successfully and to be aware that many skills can be achieved at different levels. When a student says, '*Oh, I can do that*' you need to find out at what level of competence. It may be necessary to show the student that a higher level of competence is required in a particular context.

Compare: '*I was a journalist in Turkey. I speak Turkish, Kurdish and French. I can type*' and

19

'I worked as a journalist for five years in Turkey writing for a regional newspaper. I speak fluent Turkish and Kurdish and am quite good at French. I have excellent typing skills and am learning word processing.'

Much of the accreditation available in further education is competence based. Competences are about skills that people can do. Accreditation such as the RSA ESOL Profile or City and Guilds Communication Skills (Wordpower) lists the skills and competences required and describes the levels. These may be useful in devising a programme, whether or not a student wishes to enter for the Certificate. Wordpower, however, is a Basic Skills Certificate not designed specifically for ESOL students. It concentrates on literacy skills and oral skills and may need developing further for ESOL students. There is more on accreditation in Chapter 9.

3. Assessing the student's current competence in the four language skills

The initial interview, if conducted in English, may be adequate in itself as a means of assessing listening and speaking skills. People can usually speak about themselves to some extent, feel confident about giving this kind of information and, of course, it is always appropriate.

The interview is a flexible method as it can be pitched at different levels. If a student has only given short answers and not shown whether s/he can speak more extensively, you can ask her/him to expand on some points. When assessing listening skills remember that a student may understand more than the level of the responses to the questions suggest. Reading and filling in a form together will give some information about a student's literacy skills.

In addition to the initial interview you will need to set tasks in each language skill in order to give more precise information about a student's language needs. These tasks should be carried out at a separate time from the initial interview. They should be chosen with care to suit the individual as far as possible. They should not take the form of formal tests and should be done in a collaborative, supportive way to give a student confidence. They should be accessible in format. In other words, they should not use exercise techniques which might be unfamiliar and would need practice to carry out successfully.

The kinds of task you might do are:

Speaking:
- describing a picture or sequence of pictures
- describing a personal experience
- giving instructions, e.g. safety rules, how to cook something, how to use a machine
- talking about ideas, e.g. political, social, cultural, an aspect of a college course
- a simple role-play, e.g. asking for something in a shop, making an appointment, asking for a day off work.

Listening:
- listening to a story and sequencing pictures
- listening to and carrying out instructions.

Reading:
- self assessment on a range of texts
- reading one text at an appropriate level and answering oral or written questions.

Writing:
- writing or copying personal information in sentences
- writing about reasons for wanting English lessons
- writing the story or instructions listened to previously
- writing a note or a letter.

Subsequent chapters will focus on identifying a student's language needs from the assessment procedure.

4. Negotiating a programme

When all this information has been obtained you can then discuss with the student what the priority areas are and plan a programme with specific objectives for a specified period of time, such as five weeks or 20 hours, as appropriate. You should set a date to review progress and outcomes and plan the next stage of learning, if necessary. Some goals can be achieved in a short time while others may have to be worked towards in stages over a long period of time.

A beginner student is likely to rely on you to provide guidance and devise a structured programme which will give her/him the basic tools of the language.

Further reading

Open Learning and ESOL – Liz Voss, ALBSU 1991. This gives a more detailed description of planning, assessing and reviewing procedures.

Initial interview and assessment in ESOL, Nancy Rowbottom, ALBSU Newsletter No.34, 1989.

Assessing bi-lingual adults for training, Ann Simpson, ALBSU Newsletter, No.39, 1990.

Building a Framework, Jean McAllister and Margaret Robson, National Extension College (NEC) 1984.

Assessment of Prior Learning, Noyona Chanda, ALBSU Newsletter, No.37, 1990.

A New Way to Train, Margaret Robson, 'Go To Work on Your English', Series, NEC 1990.

ESOL Initial Assessment Pack, Jane Jordan, Stockport ESOL Unit, Davenport Centre, Stockport, Cheshire 1990.

Teaching ESOL, ALBSU 1992. A video for new tutors, focussing on listening and speaking skills.

3 | Language Awareness

This chapter examines the important elements that need to be considered when teaching English and how they are used. These are:

1. **The Four Language Skills**   3. **Grammar**   5. **Pronunciation**
2. **Functions**   4. **Vocabulary**   6. **Spelling and punctuation.**

If you plan to teach English it is essential that you are or become aware of how the language works. It is not enough that you can speak English yourself.

1. The Four Language Skills

The four language skills are listening, speaking, reading and writing. They can be divided into oral and written skills or receptive (listening and reading) and productive (speaking and writing). The crucial factor in the receptive skills is understanding. The productive skills are more difficult and therefore often less advanced than their receptive equivalent.

In teaching, especially in the early stages, the skills are usually presented in the following order: listening, speaking, reading, writing. In reality the balance of the skills varies according to the context. When devising work for a particular context you need to analyse how the skills are used and how important each of them is in that context. In addition, a student may be mainly interested in practising oral skills or, on the other hand, may have good oral skills and want to concentrate on written skills.

Here is an example of an analysis made of the language skills used in a real situation.

Context: **Telephoning to order office supplies.**	
Listening • Carefully to precise details, prices, sizes, etc., some technical details difficult to understand.	*Speaking* • Asking to be put through to correct department. • Saying what I wanted. • Asking for information on prices and quantities. • Asking for clarification of technical terms.
Reading • Catalogue. • Yellow Pages for numbers of suppliers.	*Writing* • Noting the details of prices, etc. • Completing a Purchase Order.
Skills in order of importance: Speaking, listening, writing, reading – but all almost equally important and essential to the task.	

2. Functions

What are functions?

Describing language in terms of functions is a way of classifying language according to meaning. A language function means the purpose for which the language is used. If you look at the analysis of the two contexts you will see that the descriptions of what was done under each skill are in terms of functions.

Asking for directions:	*Can you tell me where . . . ?*
Giving directions:	*They're in the third aisle on the left.*
Requesting:	*Can you put me through to office supplies, please?*
Asking for information:	*How much are the . . . ?*
Giving information:	*They're £20 a dozen.*

There are a large number of language functions which can be grouped as follows:

Giving and asking for factual information is a major function which can be sub-divided into:

- identifying – *'My name is . . .'*, *'He is a (student)'*, *'This is a . . .'*, *'Who is . . .?'*, *'What is . . .?'*
- describing (objects, people, places, feelings)
- describing routines, processes
- narrating (past events)
- describing recent events and experiences
- describing future plans and events
- instructing.

Social interaction:
- greeting and introducing people
- requesting
- inviting
- suggesting, etc.

Attitudes:
- apologising
- giving opinions
- agreeing
- expressing preferences, etc.

Functions and contexts

If you start thinking in this way about the language you use in different contexts you will find that the *same* functions are used in many *different* contexts. This has important implications for language teaching.

Function: **Narrating**	
Context	**Example**
Social	*We had a lovely weekend. We went to my cousin's wedding.*
Work	*I fitted a new clutch this morning.*
Study	*I handed in my essay yesterday.*
At the doctor's	*I had back trouble a few years ago.*

This means that if you teach your student how to express a function in one context s/he can transfer that learning to another context.

Ways of expressing functions

It is also true that the same function can be expressed in different ways and to differing degrees of formality.

Function: **Suggesting**		
Informal	*Let's have . . .*	
	What about having . . .	
	Why don't we have . . .	
	Shall we have . . .	*a meeting about this(?)*
	I suggest we have . . .	
Formal	*If I might make a suggestion we could have . . .*	

There can be so many ways of expressing a function it would be confusing to introduce a student to all of them! You can teach a beginner student the simplest and most generally useful way of expressing a function. Then at an intermediate level you can introduce a range of ways of expressing a function and an awareness of when to use a formal or informal style. You could also teach a student to use one or two ways but to recognise others.

You will need to identify the functions required for the contexts chosen by a student and select a way of expressing these functions appropriate to the level of the student.

Functions and grammar

Each function has particular grammatical features, vocabulary and expressions associated with it. This helps you to group teaching items in a meaningful way.

Function: **Describing**	
Language	**Example**
Statements often in Present Simple tense The verbs, BE, HAVE (GOT) IS MADE OF	*I feel sick* *She's got a headache* *The container is round* *It has a lid* *It's made of plastic*
Adjectives Frequency	*These toys are colourful* *He usually goes to work by train*
Prepositional phrases	*next to the bank, the* *woman with glasses.*
Measurements There is (a) There are (some)	*6 feet tall* *There's a pen in the drawer* *There are some spanners over there*

3. Grammar

What is grammar?

Grammar is the nuts and bolts of language. When people pick up a language informally they usually find it easy to learn essential vocabulary but much harder to put sentences together grammatically. They can get their meaning across and become quite fluent using their own 'system'. Incorrect usage becomes a habit and what are often called 'fossilised errors' develop. It is like having all the bits of self-assembly furniture but no instructions as to how to put it together. Some students come to ESOL programmes because they are aware of this and want to learn to use the language correctly.

Some of the links between functions and grammar have already been described.

Grammatical features are used to express other concepts such as:

- the timing of an action: e.g. *I work, I worked, I have worked*
- number: e.g. *book/books; glass/glasses; child/children; it/they, is/are*
- the subject: e.g. *I, we, he, she*
- the object: e.g. *me, them, us*
- possession: e.g. *my, our, his, their, John's*
- whether something is specific or not: i.e. **a** *student,* **the** *Prime Minister.*

Grammar is also about structure. It means knowing how to put the language together, what can go with what, the order of words.

Word order is very important in English. In the sentence, *'A man attacked two girls*

25

in the park.' English relies on the order of words to show who attacked whom. Word order is fairly rigid in English with few possible variations. Try adding *'brutally'*, *'teenage'*, *'last night'* to the above sentence and think where you could or could not put them. You know that *'This computer is much cheaper'* is a possible sentence in English, while *'This computer much is cheaper'* is not. The change of word order to indicate a question is an important structural feature. *'She has finished her assignment.'* *'Has she finished her assignment yet?'*.

This fixed word order enables you to build up sentence patterns where different words can be slotted in to a particular framework.

Who?	did what?	where?		when?
I	walked	to	the shops	this morning.
He	drove	to	the airport	this afternoon.
They	arrived	at	the station	this evening.

Learning sentence patterns helps a student to be aware of word order and to make up other sentences following the same pattern.

The mother tongue and English

It is important to remember that ESOL students have already learned at least one other language. The similarities and differences between the mother tongue and English may, on the one hand, help learning by the transfer of knowledge and, on the other hand, may hinder learning because different habits have been formed.

Compare how this sentence is expressed in different languages.

	1	2	3	4	5
	I	*work*	*in*	*an*	*office*
Urdu:	1	5	3	_____2_____	
(transcription)	*mai*	*daftar*	*me*	*kam karta* (m) *huũ* *karti* (f)	
Vietnamese:	1	2	3	5	
	Tôi	*làm việc*	*trong*	*văn*	*phòng*
Spanish	1	2	3	4	5
	Yo	*trabajo*	*en*	*una*	*oficina*

Urdu: Different word order. Masculine and feminine forms of the verb. Three words to express *work*. No equivalent of *an*.

Vietnamese: Same word order. No equivalent of *an*. Two words for *work*. Two words for *office*.

Spanish: Word order the same. Equivalence for each word.

The place of grammar and functions for ESOL teachers and students

It is essential to tackle these aspects of language teaching. In fact you cannot teach language without teaching grammar. The question is, rather, whether you teach grammar explicitly, by explaining the rules, or implicitly, by example. In either case plenty of practice is necessary for learning to take place. A student's level, educational background and whether you can use the mother tongue will determine your approach to grammar. A beginner is usually taught through example and practice. A student like **Omer** (profiled in Chapter 1), who has already learned another language in a formal way may well find it useful to be given some rules and explanations.

All ESOL teachers need a knowledge of grammar and functions to be able to select and organise the items to teach in a coherent and effective way. A knowledge of grammatical terms, while not essential, gives useful labels for reference. Some knowledge of the similarities and differences between a student's mother tongue and English can enable you to help a student transfer knowledge and alert you to possible difficulties.

A student needs to develop understanding of English grammar and functions either implicitly or explicitly in order to transfer language learnt in one context to another.

For example, if a student learns a dialogue in a particular context without developing an understanding of the elements that make up the dialogue, s/he may know some phrases for that one situation but will be unable to transfer that learning to other situations. It is a 'phrase book' approach.

If students know some of the similarities and differences between their mother tongue and English it can help their understanding of English and make them aware of aspects they need to learn.

4. Vocabulary

What is vocabulary?

Vocabulary means words. Words can initially be divided into two main groups:

1. The first is a small group consisting of little words that are used frequently in all contexts and which give structure to the sentence. They have little meaning in isolation. Such words are: '*the, a, this, that, you, it, they, them, me, some, to, in, at, and, but*', etc.

It is very important to know these words and how they are used, as once learned they can be used in many different situations. (These words are sometimes called *structural* words).

2. The second group is extremely large and consists of words that carry a lot of meaning in isolation, such as: *'student, teacher, book, pen, learn, write, clever, carefully'*, i.e. nouns, verbs, adjectives, adverbs. These words are the ones that can create a context. They present a big learning load for a student as each context has its own specific vocabulary, although, of course, many words have a wide general usage. (These words are sometimes called *content* words).

Teaching vocabulary

When people talk about teaching vocabulary they usually mean words from the second group. It is useful to teach vocabulary on a thematic basis to link in with the context that has been selected. However, at times you may wish to group words according to:

- grammatical function: *in; on; at; near:*
  often, usually, sometimes, never
  read, write, study, learn.
- sound/spelling relationship: *eat, dear, meat.*
- how they are built up: *beautiful, careful, wonderful*
  economic, uneconomic, economist.

5. Pronunciation

What kind of pronunciation?

If a student says, *'I want to learn to speak English properly'* or *'People don't understand me'* there may be a need for the student to improve her/his pronunciation. However, first of all you need to identify what the difficulties are. There may not, in fact, be a significant problem with pronunciation. The student may simply be worried about having an accent and thinks it is necessary to aim at what is perceived as Standard English. The student may need reassuring that having a different accent is perfectly acceptable as long as it is comprehensible to the listener.

English is an international language and there are many varieties of spoken English: Welsh, Scottish, Yorkshire, American, Caribbean, Indian, etc. No one of them is the 'correct' one. People who start learning another language as adults are very unlikely to achieve 'native speaker' pronunciation unless they have a very good ear for language. This does not matter. What does matter is that their pronunciation does not impede understanding. If this is the case they will lose confidence and be afraid to speak.

What is pronunciation?

When you listen to someone speaking you do not really hear the individual sounds.

One sound merges with the next one and one word with the next. Some words have a lot of weight put on them and others hardly any. The voice rises and falls.

e.g. *When'reyougoingout?*

When teaching pronunciation there are four aspects to consider:

(a) sounds

(b) stress and rhythm

(c) intonation

(d) fluency

(a) Sounds

There are 44 sounds in English: 24 consonant sounds, 12 vowels and 8 diphthongs (2 vowel sounds together). A student will have learnt another set of sounds for his/her mother tongue. Where there are equivalent sounds there will be no problems. There is only likely to be difficulty where English sounds do not exist in the mother tongue or where they are not used in the same combination. Sounds are produced differently at the beginning, middle and ends of words and some sounds can only be used in certain positions. For example the sound 'ng' cannot be used at the beginning of a word in English. Languages differ in the combinations possible and some consonant clusters such as *school, stream, film, crisps* can be difficult for some speakers so that they tend to put in an extra vowel, e.g. *sikool* or miss a sound out, e.g. *crips*.

Mispronunciation of a sound usually only becomes significant if it is confused with another sound. There are many words in English where only one sound distinguishes it from another word. These are called minimal pairs. Such pairs are: *fill/feel, nice/rice, tree/three*. Here an inability to produce these sounds differently may cause misunderstandings, although as they will be spoken in a context this will help the listener understand which word is intended. In Hindi 'p' is used for both 'f' and 'p' so *feel/peel, fill/pill* may be confused. Similarly 'e' and 'a' are not clearly distinguished as in *pet/pat*. Long vowels tend to be made short so a misunderstanding, if only momentarily, like the following can occur:

STUDENT: *I haven't got any pepper*

TEACHER: *Pardon?* (Thinks: What does she want pepper for?)

STUDENT: *I haven't got any pepper to write on.*

TUTOR: *Oh! paper! Yes, here you are. Now, can you say, payper?*

Sounds omitted at the ends of words can also make a person difficult to understand. Cantonese speakers have problems with final consonant sounds. 'b', 'd', 'g' do not occur at the ends of words and are confused with 'p', 't', 'k'. These are also very lightly sounded and may not be heard by the listener. Even though consonant sounds are not sounded at the end of a word as they are at the beginning, the sound is nevertheless there. The way the 't' is sounded at the beginning and end of 'tent' illustrates this.

(b) Stress and Rhythm

This is the beat of the language. There are two types of stress; (a) word stress and (b) sentence stress.

(a) *Word stress.* In words of two syllables or more one syllable is stressed more than the other(s). This is invariable and is best learnt when the word is first taught. English tends to stress the first syllable but of course there are many variations, e.g. *training, college, trainee, computer, application, apply.* There are pairs like '*I refuse to do this*', and '*Leave your refuse here*', where the noun is stressed on the first syllable and the verb on the last syllable. The meanings can be quite different as in this example or connected as in '*Prices will increase*' and '*An increase in prices is likely*'. A few words have alternative stress patterns, e.g. *controversy* and *controversy.*

(b) Sentence stress. Within a sentence some words are stressed and others are unstressed. The stressed words or syllables are timed fairly evenly giving English its characteristic rhythm. The structural words tend to be unstressed and the words with more meaning stressed, e.g. '*She took her exam last week.* When words are unstressed they are pronounced with a shorter sound and often contracted, e.g. *I am → I'm, he will → he'll, 'I'm sure she'll pass.'*

Sometimes we give extra stress to a particular word in a sentence to give a special meaning. Almost any word can be stressed this way. For example:

I don't live in Manchester. (but she does).

I don't live in Manchester. (but I work there).

Each language has its own stress patterns so a student may find it difficult to adapt to the stress patterns of English.

(c) Intonation

This is the tune of the language. The way the voice rises and falls conveys meaning and feelings. Other languages use different intonation patterns; some are spoken almost on a level and in others, like Cantonese and Mandarin, the meaning of a word changes according to the tone or pitch.

In English there are many possible intonation patterns to show different moods and attitudes but for beginners it is best to concentrate on the two main tunes. These are:

(i) the low fall, and (ii) the low rise, i.e. The voice falls or rises slightly on the last stressed syllable of a sentence.

(i) The falling tune is used for statements, commands and questions beginning with a question word, e.g. '*What's the time?*' '*It's half past three.*'

(ii) The rising tune is used for requests and questions expecting the answer '*yes*' or '*no*', e.g. '*Are you going now?*' '*Could you turn the light off, please?*'

Sharper rises and falls indicate stronger feelings and attitudes.

If students do not recognise English intonation patterns they will be unable to pick up the signals which say, *'I'm asking a question'* or *'I'm angry'*. Similarly they will be unable to convey these signals. Using the wrong stress and intonation patterns can often make a student harder to understand than making the sounds wrongly. It can also make someone sound abrupt and rude.

This diagram shows the main intonation patterns in English.

Low fall	High fall	Low rise	High rise	Fall rise	Rise fall
↘	↘	↗	↗	∿	↘
Definite (Statements, Commands question-word questions)	Definite Strong commands, Enthusiasm	Query Politeness (Yes/no questions Requests)	Surprise Disbelief	Doubt Hesitation	Sarcasm Humour

Based on Home Tutor Handbook, Natesla, CRE

(d) Fluency

This means the smooth transition between one word and the next and the speaking in phrase groups rather than word-by-word. If a student does not blend one word with the next s/he sounds stilted.

For example: I | am | going | for | an | interview | tomorrow. |

instead of: *'I'm going for an interview tomorrow.'*

In conclusion, listen carefully to identify the problem areas and only deal with those that interfere with comprehension. An awareness of the differences between a student's mother tongue and English will help.

6. Spelling and punctuation

Spelling

The written form of the language attemps to represent the sounds made in the spoken language. In some languages a letter or group of letters consistently represents the same sound, in other words they are written phonetically. In English, however, particularly in relation to vowel sounds there are various ways of spelling the same sound, e.g. *vain, vane, vein* and the same spelling can have different sounds, e.g. *meat, head*. Sometimes the spelling is more related to meaning than sound, e.g. words that sound the same like *sun* and *son* are distinguished by their spelling. An advantage of having a spelling system not always directly related to sound is that one spelling of a word can represent different pronunciations.

Pronunciation, of course, will affect spelling as a student is likely to spell words as s/he pronounces them. Students who use the same alphabet as English will also find that the different sound values given to the letters in the mother tongue influence both spelling and pronunciation in English. A student who is used to a phonetically written language may feel frustrated at the vagaries of English spelling.

Punctuation

Punctuation makes a text easier to read by breaking it up. Some punctuation rules are to do with grammar and some with meaning. Some represent the information conveyed by pauses, falling and rising intonations, etc., in the spoken language. For example, at the end of a sentence you may drop your voice and take a breath. When you write you put a full stop and start again with a capital letter. The conventions in other languages may be different and the system in English may have to be learnt, e.g. in some languages where a different script is used there are no capital letters. Some ESOL students find it difficult to identify the end of a sentence and where to put the full stop.

The diagram below illustrates the aspects of language described in this chapter.

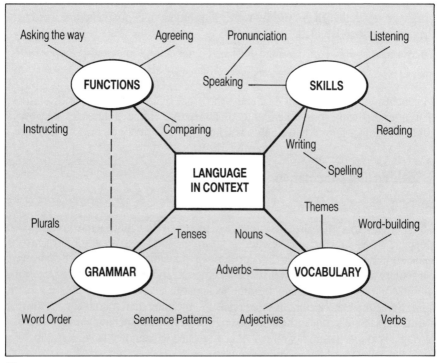

Further reading

Awareness of Language: An introduction, E. Hawkins, Cambridge University Press 1987.

A Communicative Grammar of English, G. Leech and J. Svartvik, Longman 1975.

Discover English, Bolitho and Tomlinson, Heinemann 1981.

An Introduction to English Grammar, Sidney Greenbaum, London 1991 (includes sections on spelling and punctuation).

Practical English Grammar, A.J. Thomson and A.V. Martinet, Longman (4th ed.) 1986.

Practical English Usage, Michael Swan, Oxford University Press 1980.

Threshold Level English, J.A. van Ek and L.G. Alexander, Pergamon Press 1980.

A very simple grammar of English, C. Blisset and K. Hallgarten, Language Teaching Publications 1985.

An A-Z of English Grammar and Usage, Geoffrey Leech, Nelson.

Better English Pronunciation, J.D. O'Connor, Cambridge University Press 1980 ed.

Learner English, Michael Swan and Bernard Smith, Cambridge University Press 1987.

Sounds English, J.D. O'Connor and Clare Fletcher, Longman 1989.

Spelling It Out, Rhiannedd Pratley, BBC 1988.

4 | Planning a Programme – 2

The last chapter examined the language elements you should be aware of when assessing and teaching a student. This chapter will look at ways of putting these elements together into a learning programme or syllabus and identifying spoken language needs and incorporating them into a learning programme by focusing on an individual student.

What approach is suitable for ESOL students?

As ESOL students need to use English in their everyday lives and for specific purposes it is not usually appropriate to follow a strictly sequenced grammatical or functional syllabus.

A beginner student certainly needs a syllabus that covers the basic structures within relevant contexts. However, there needs to be flexibility about the order in which structures are taught to account for individual needs. It is no good if the language a student wants to use at the shops or the parents' evening comes in Lesson 25 of a course s/he has just started.

Most ESOL students have already learned some English, maybe formally in classes in their country of origin or informally by listening to and using the language in everyday life. Their knowledge of the language will be unpredictable according to their experience. In one context they may be able to use quite an advanced level of English, while in another they may not know quite basic vocabulary. They do not want to spend time on a course doing things they can do already.

Therefore a suitable approach for ESOL students is a learning programme based on language competences in terms of the skills, functions, grammar and vocabulary which a student needs to learn to achieve the goals already identified. It is also necessary to try and grade the language so that it is within reach of a student. A student who can already do some of the competences will have this prior learning credited and will practise the language and skills needed to achieve the competences s/he cannot do. Some intermediate level students who want to improve their accuracy may need a syllabus that practises basic grammatical structures but in a way which takes account of the level of vocabulary and fluency already acquired.

The aim of ESOL is to develop the required competence at the right level as quickly as possible. Setting manageable targets helps towards this end and some goals can be achieved quickly. However, it must be said that some competences can take a long time to achieve; for example 'describing a past experience' involves lot of work with tenses that can take months if not years to be able to use proficiently. You may also need to encourage a student not to aim for perfect English before s/he feels able to go and try something new.

Planning a programme for an individual student

Identifying spoken language needs

When you have identified the main learning goals with a student and analysed the skills and language needed to achieve these goals the student's current level of competence needs to be assessed in order to identify what aspects of language need to be worked on.

First of all select some appropriate tasks for a student in order to assess listening and speaking skills. In Chapter 2 some activities were suggested for this more detailed stage of assessment. As the student is speaking note down how successful communication has been, as well as any problem areas, using these headings:

- **Functions**
- **Grammar**
- **Vocabulary**
- **Pronunciation**

It can be helpful to record the student if s/he is happy about this so you can both listen and identify successful communication and errors.

Then agree on the priority items especially in relation to the goals and skills you have already discussed.

Here is an example of part of an oral assessment of **Ladda,** (one of the students profiled in Chapter 1) and a sample plan to show how the teaching items identified could be incorporated into the student's learning programme.

Assessment of Needs

Since coming to Britain **Ladda** has already learned a considerable amount of English. When she joined the ESOL workshop she had an initial interview and a broad assessment of her existing skills and her main learning goals were identified and entered on her planning chart. The tutor had already begun to identify some of **Ladda's** specific language needs. The tutor then asked her to carry out some oral tasks to find out more about her language competence. Here is a transcription of part of the assessment with tutor comments.

Analysis

The communication was generally successful.

Functions:

Giving information in answer to question – successful except she did not pick up the *'How do you like . . .?*

Describing a routine – successful, good sequencing, some correct verb forms.

Grammar:

Not clear about usage of present simple (*I clean*) and present continuous (*I am cleaning*). Needs to use the present simple for a routine. Incorrect form of present continuous – omission of *'am'*.

Wrong use of *'have been'*.

Omission of *'at'* with time.

Uncertain about singular and plural – *the table(s), a cup (the cups)*.

Word order – successful but *'5 days a week, 3 hours a day'*.

Vocabulary:

Quite adequate for the task. Note: come/go.

Pronunciation:

Clear. Easy to understand on the whole. *'v'* sound – *'five days'* sounded like *'Friday'*. *'th'* in *'then'* like *'d'*. *'six'* like *'sik'*, *'f'* for *'p'* in *'cup'*. Rising intonation at end of every sentence makes her sound questioning and surprised.

PLANNING CHART

Name: ...... Ladda .... Date ....

Tutor's name: ....

Initial Assessment

Level of English:

Listening: ...Good understanding of interview questions...............

Speaking: ..Can give personal information without difficulty.
Quite fluent. Errors eg. tenses.......................................

Reading: ..Can read words on form. High frequency words......
Can try unfamiliar words. Reads slowly word by word.......

Writing: ..Prints clearly. Can fill in form with help in spelling
some words...

Personal Goals:

..English for work as waitress...

..Improve grammar..

..Social talk with in-laws and people at work.......................

..Making appointments and talking to the doctor.................

Priority goal: ..English for work as waitress.........................

Skills/knowledge	Can do	Needs to do
Checking and taking bookings		✓
Showing to table	✓	
offering drinks etc.	✓	
Taking orders	✓	more practice - polite.
Suggesting		✓ forms - intonation
Giving information about food		✓
Dealing with a complaint		
Reading menu	✓	✓ more difficult words
Writing orders (using numbers)	✓	

Assessed needs ..Polite forms for offering etc..........................
Pronunciation - of food items, number (five, six), days of week. -
Sounds: 'v', 'p' 'f' 'th' 'at' + time. Tenses: I work / am working.
I worked / have worked. I'll work. Question forms Plurals: - adding -s

37

Incorporating the needs into the learning programme

Overleaf is a planning chart showing how **Ladda's** goals and language needs were recorded.

The tutor and Ladda then agreed on a learning programme which concentrated on the priority goal and included the assessed needs. This would also go some way to meeting the second goal as grammatical items would be dealt with. Remember this outline is for guidance and can be modified. Some items may prove easy for **Ladda** and be done more quickly than expected, others may take longer and need extra practice. Additional needs will be identified and added to the programme.

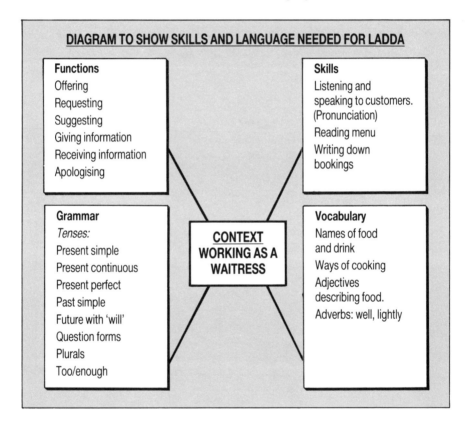

DIAGRAM TO SHOW SKILLS AND LANGUAGE NEEDED FOR LADDA

Functions
Offering
Requesting
Suggesting
Giving information
Receiving information
Apologising

Skills
Listening and speaking to customers. (Pronunciation)
Reading menu
Writing down bookings

Grammar
Tenses:
Present simple
Present continuous
Present perfect
Past simple
Future with 'will'
Question forms
Plurals
Too/enough

CONTEXT WORKING AS A WAITRESS

Vocabulary
Names of food and drink
Ways of cooking
Adjectives describing food.
Adverbs: well, lightly

Further reading

Open Learning and ESOL, Liz Voss, ALBSU 1991

Syllabus Design, David Nunan, Oxford University Press 1988.

ESOL Syllabus Design, Ed. Patty Hemmingway, Language & Literacy Unit, Southwark 1989.

A LEARNING PROGRAMME

Targets To pronounce items on menu clearly
To pronounce numbers clearly for menu and prices
To learn new vocabulary for food and ways of cooking
To describe ingredients and how dishes are cooked
To practise offering, suggesting, apologising
To understand complaints
To describe work routine using present simple and "at" + time. To
ask questions for information. To state intention

Session 1 Describe work routine - present simple, times
Greeting customers. Questions: Have you booked? What name?
How many people?
Polite requests: Please wait a moment. Please come this
way. Practise reading and saying items on menu. Practise numbers

Session 2 Offering: Would you like a ——?
Listening to orders, identifying on menu, writing numbers. Taking an order
dialogue - concentrate on pronunciation. Present perfect: Have you booked/
ordered/finished? Describing food rich, spicy, hot, tender etc.
a/an some. Singular/plural: glass/glasses, plate/plates

Session 3 Describe ingredients: answering, "What's in it?"
Describe ways of cooking. It's fried, boiled etc.
it is/They are.
Dialogue with customer. Role-play
Choose favourite dish and describe or write how to make it

Session 4 Questions. Do you like ....?
Suggesting: formal. I suggest you have .... Listening to
complaints. Identifying the problem — use of 'too'
(not) enough, very. Apologising. Stating intention:
I'll change it. I'll get another. I'll call the manager.

Materials

Menu   Pictures of food   Taped dialogues   Worksheets

Role-play card: (Basic Listening Unit 9 [Ordering a meal];
Tree or Three? pronunciation; Essential Grammar in Use).

5 | Developing Listening Skills

The previous chapters have been concerned with identifying needs and planning a learning programme. This chapter begins to look at teaching methods by examining ways of developing listening skills. It considers what is involved in listening, the teacher's use of language and how to practise listening with a student.

1. The importance of listening

You have to listen to a language before you can speak it. It is the basis upon which all the other language skills are built. Listening to English is the principal way learners of English get information both about the language and about the situations within which they will be using English. It is important at all levels from beginner to advanced. In any teaching situation, whether it is 1:1. in a group, in the workplace or in a college, a student must be able to listen effectively to learn. In some methods of teaching students spend a long time listening to the language before they are expected to speak. You can also encourage students to listen actively outside the classroom. When they are listening to the radio or TV, or to friends or colleagues talking they can extend their knowledge of English by mentally noting words, phrases, expressions and tone. They can practise the listening skills learnt in the classroom.

2. Listening in everyday life

What and who do we listen to?

In Chapters 2 and 3 some listening tasks students might have to do in 'real life' and some ways listening skills are used in different contexts were outlined.

As well as understanding you, students may need to understand other teachers, administrative staff, officials, public announcements, people on the telephone, television or radio programmes, supervisors, friends and workmates. Sometimes listening simply involves receiving the information (monologue, e.g. a broadcast, lecture, announcement) and sometimes it involves responding to it (conversation, dialogue, discussion).

Why do we listen?

We listen with different purposes and with differing levels of concentration according to what is being listened to and how interested we are in it. If we are listening to a set of instructions we listen carefully to every word because it is all important. Sometimes we just want to get specific factual information and listen only for that (e.g. the time of a train, the platform it leaves from), so we ignore the rest of the information. If we are listening to a friend telling a story we may listen to the gist of it because the details are not important to us. At other times picking up the mood of the other person is most important – s/he is angry, upset, frightened, happy.

How do we listen and understand?

Of course, we have to be able to understand most of the language, the vocabulary and the structure, but other things help as well. When people speak it is usually unscripted, not prepared in advance, so there is a lot of what is called redundant language. This means hesitations, repetition, going off the point. If we are listening for gist we try to select the main points or key words. Tone, stress and intonation give us more clues. Non-verbal communication, such as gestures and facial expression, can also be very helpful. Think how much more difficult it is understanding people on the telephone. Finally, context is a crucial element in understanding: the place you hear the language in, the person you are listening to, things around you, other visual clues such as maps, diagrams, notices.

3. Teacher language

In the teaching situation you have control over the language a student listens to. The main person s/he will listen to is you. As it is important that a student understands you, you need to think carefully about the language you use and how you say it. Make sure that when you give instructions to a student you use language at the right level. If you are bi-lingual think what is best said in the mother tongue and what in English. Here are some guidelines to help you:

- Speak clearly and for beginner and elementary students slightly more slowly.
- Speak naturally without distorting rhythm and intonation.
- Use the normal contractions of colloquial speech, e.g. I've, he's, it's, you've, etc.
- Pause between sentences not words.
- Repeat your original sentence two or three times if the student does not understand at first. S/he may simply need time to process the information.
- Only paraphrase if you realise that that you have used language which is too difficult.
- Teach the student useful phrases; '*I'm sorry I don't understand,*' '*Please can you say it again,*' '*What does that word mean?*'
- Do not speak for too long without checking understanding.
- Make a clear distinction between the language you use to instruct the student and the language items you are teaching.

- Use visual materials, real objects, gestures and actions to create context and illustrate meaning.

Using the mother tongue

If you can speak a student's mother tongue, even to a small extent, it can be very useful. Use the mother tongue to avoid long complicated explanations, to check for meaning or understanding, to explain an activity. However, presentation of new structures and vocabulary should be in English and it is also useful for a student to learn the langauge of instruction in English. As your lesson may be the student's only experience of learning English in a structured way it is essential to maximise her/his exposure to English.

Here is an example of a tutor giving instructions in English at two levels:

(i) Beginner

Teach simple instruction words. Use gestures to convey the meaning to start with.

T. Look at the picture *(point)*. There're two people. They're in a shop. What kind of shop is it?

S. Fruit and . . . and . . . What is potato?

T. Potatoes. They're vegetables.

S. Yes. Vegetables.

T. It's a greengrocer's. It sells fruit and vegetables. This is the shop assistant and this is Naseem. She buys some fruit and vegetables.

Listen *(point to ear)*. Tell me *(point to mouth)* what she buys. *(Point to pictures of items and name them)*. Apples, potatoes, carrots, tomatoes. Listen *(play tape)*. What does she buy?

S. *(Points to picture)*. Tomato.

T. Good. Tomatoes. You say it. *(point to mouth)*. Tomatoes.

S. Tomatoes.

Tapescript

Shopkeeper: Good morning. What would you like?

Customer: Good morning. I'd like a pound of tomatoes, please.

Shopkeeper: Right. The tomatoes are very nice this week. Anything else?

Customer: No thanks. That's all. How much is that?

Shopkeeper: 60p

Customer: Here you are.

Shopkeeper: Thanks. Goodbye.

Customer: Goodbye

(Based on 'A New Start', Furnborough et al, Heinemann)

(ii) Elementary to intermediate

Keep the instructions clear and simple. You can rely more on the language but still point to the sections the student has to fill in or tick. At this level the tapescript would be longer with the shopper buying more items. Choose the appropriate weight system.

> 'Now I'm going to play you a tape. You'll hear two people talking. They're in a shop. One is the shopkeeper and the other is the customer. Listen and tick the things the customer buys. (*point to worksheet*). (*Play tape*). Now listen again and check your answers. This time put a circle round how much she buys, like this. (*Point to example on worksheet*). Put a circle round how much she spends altogether. (*Point to list of prices on worksheet.*) Are you ready? (*Play tape again*)'.

LISTENING   SHOPPING   ELEMENTARY

1) LISTEN   Tick what the shopper buys   ☑

2) LISTEN   Circle how much or how many she buys   (1lb)

apples	☐	½ kg / 1lb	1kg / 2lbs	1½ kg / 3lbs
bananas	☐	3	4	6
oranges	☐	4	6	8
carrots	☐	½ kg / 1lb	1kg / 2lbs	2 kg / 4lbs
mushrooms	☐	125 gms / ¼ lb	200 gms / 6ozs	250 gms / ½ lb
lettuce	☐	1	2	3
tomatoes	☐	250 gms / ½ lb	½ kg / 1lb	750 gms / 1½ lb

3) How much does she spend altogether?

£3.50   £3.15   £4.25   £4.50

4. What materials can you use?

Outside the classroom there is no way of controlling the English that a student has to listen to. Therefore you must train a student to listen effectively even when s/he does not understand everything. Students often need encouraging to believe that they do not, in fact, have to understand every word someone says to be able to get the main points. Nevertheless the listening material needs to be within the grasp of a student. It is no good if there is too much unknown language.

- You can tape short pieces of authentic spoken English of the type a student wants to be able to listen to. Authentic means it is 'real' language, not specially prepared for teaching: for example, an extract from the radio or TV news, some friends discussing a topic, an instructor demonstrating how to do something. You can use video too if you have the facilities.

- You can tape your own specially prepared materials; for example, a dialogue with a hairdresser, a job interview, a set of instructions, a story. This way you can make sure the material is the right level for a student but remember to include some repetition and hesitations and some unknown words as well.

- You can select appropriate material from commercially prepared books and cassettes. These are usually graded for different levels which can be helpful. They try to be as authentic as possible but sometimes can sound rather artificial.

By providing a range of listening materials you can give a student the chance not just to listen to you but to different voices and accents.

5. How to present listening exercises to a student

- First of all prepare the student for what s/he is to hear. Prediction helps understanding. Set the scene. Teach any necessary vocabulary.

- As we usually listen with a purpose in mind tell the student in advance what you want her/him to listen for, either orally or in the form of pre-listening questions.

- Give the student a task that will check understanding. (See list opposite).

- Play the tape once and ask for the student's self assessment. Could s/he understand it well, a bit, not at all?

- Play the tape several times until the student can pick out the required information or make the required responses.

- Play the tape in sections to focus on a little bit at a time.

- Encourage the student to work out or guess difficult bits.

- Encourage the student to make notes in English or in the mother tongue or to give mother tongue explanations if appropriate.

- Instil confidence by drawing attention to the language the student can understand relatively easily.

- When the student feels secure in understanding play the whole tape through again.

6. Checking understanding

It is never enough to say, *'Do you understand?'* A student may say *'Yes'* out of politeness or because s/he thinks s/he does, while in fact s/he doesn't. If a student does not have good reading and writing skills it is best to use methods of checking that do not involve using these skills. Some methods for checking understanding are:

- Carrying out an action.
- Marking places on a map or diagram.
- Drawing.
- Identifying pictures.
- Sequencing pictures.
- Answering oral questions.
- Retelling the story – if you have used video you can turn the sound down and ask the student to provide the commentary.
- Identifying the mood and attitude of the speakers from tone and body language (if using a video).
- Selecting from multiple choice answers.

If you speak a student's language some of these activities can be done in the mother tongue as the main aim is to check understanding and not to practise speaking.

7. Examples of the types of listening materials you can use

(a) Listening for detail

This is one of the most intensive kinds of listening.

(i) Ask the student to carry out some instructions.

- Press the 'eject' button to open the lid.
- Put the cassette in the recorder.
- Close the lid firmly.
- Press the 'play' tape
- Listen to the tape.
- Press the 'stop' button.
- Press the 'fast forward' button to go forward.
- Press the 'stop' button again.
- Press the 'rewind' button to go back to the beginning.
- Press the 'eject' button.
- Take the cassette out of the recorder.

(ii) Give a set of directions and ask the student to draw the route on a map.

(b) Listening for specific information

(i) An airport announcement. The student writes down or ticks the times of arrival and departure.

(ii) A customer enquiring about prices. The student matches items and prices.

(iii) Descriptions of people or objects. The student identifies the corresponding pictures.

(iv) Making arrangements. The student notes down the day, time and place.

(c) Listening for gist/the main points

(i) People discussing an event. The student answers questions about their opinions or ticks true/false statements.

(ii) A story. The student sequences pictures or sentences.

(iii) A lecture/The news. The student identifies the main points from a list.

(iv) Social conversation. The student identifies the topics discussed.

Further reading

Active Listening, R.R. Jordan, Collins 1984 (Elementary)

Basic Listening, John McDowell and Sandra Stevens, Edward Arnold 1982 (Elementary)

Elementary Task Listening, J. St Clair Stokes, Cambridge University Press 1984.

Listening Comprehension and Note Taking, K. James, R.R. Jordan and A. Matthews, Collins (2nd ed.) 1991 (study skills – advanced).

Listening Plus, John McDowell and Christopher Hart, Edward Arnold/Nelson 1987 (intermediate to advanced).

Study Listening, Tony Lynch, Cambridge University Press, 1983 (study skills – advanced).

Task Listening, Lesley Blundell and Jackie Stokes, Cambridge University Press 1981 (Intermediate).

These are a selection of books designed for the EFL market and some of the situations may not be relevant to ESOL learners. However, the tapes provide good examples of authentic or near authentic language and the books give useful guidance on how to use the materials.

ESOL Materials

Topics and Skills in English, Vivien Barr and Clare Fletcher, Hodder and Stoughton 1983 – the taped materials from this are useful. (intermediate).

A New Start, P. Furnborough et al, Heinemann 1980 (taped materials) (beginner) Out of Print.

6 | Developing Speaking Skills

This chapter looks at a variety of ways of teaching and giving practice in spoken English including the teaching of pronunciation. It is important to remember that receptive skills (listening and reading) are always in advance of productive (speaking and writing). The distance between them varies from one individual to another according to their language experience. If a person has practised both listening and speaking from the start then the gap might be quite small. If, on the other hand, a person has had plenty of opportunity to listen to the language but not much chance or not enough confidence to practise it, then the gap might be considerable. This can be the case with some ESOL students who have lived for some time in Britain.

There are, therefore, three aims:

1. To teach new language and then give a student the opportunity to practise it. This obviously applies to beginners or near beginners but is necessary at all levels.

2. To draw out language that a student already knows but does not use very much and give her/him the confidence to use it.

3. To try and replace wrongly learnt forms with correct ones.

Methods for presenting and practising spoken language

The methods described here have been developed primarily for class teaching. However, they are equally suitable for one to one teaching with minor adaptations as necessary (e.g. only two people in a dialogue or role-play).

Presentation of new material and repetition

If you do not speak a student's language you must use a direct method presenting the English you want to teach clearly so that the student can understand. This method can be used at all levels, from beginner to advanced. With intermediate and advanced students it may also be combined with explanation and written examples.

If you can speak a student's mother tongue you can translate the key words or give a brief explanation. However, it is still essential that you repeat the English enough times for the student to grasp the new language. Too much use of the mother tongue is not helpful in the learning process.

It has already been said that a student must listen before speaking. There would also be little point in speaking without understanding.

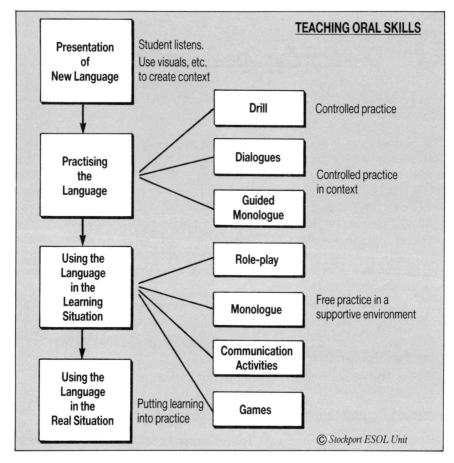

TEACHING ORAL SKILLS

Presentation of New Language — Student listens. Use visuals, etc. to create context

Practising the Language — Drill — Controlled practice; Dialogues, Guided Monologue — Controlled practice in context

Using the Language in the Learning Situation — Role-play, Monologue, Communication Activities — Free practice in a supportive environment

Using the Language in the Real Situation — Putting learning into practice — Games

© *Stockport ESOL Unit*

Therefore you must present the new language to a student so that the meaning is clear. You are not just teaching the meaning of individual words but the meaning of words in a sentence. Remember, too, that meaning is not only conveyed by words but by gesture and facial expression.

A new teaching item can be a grammatical feature (e.g. a verb tense, adding –s to make plurals), a function (e.g. complaining, inviting) or vocabulary (e.g. words on a theme: tall, short, slim, fat, pretty, plain, handsome).

Demonstrate the meaning of what you are saying by using actions, pictures or real objects. These provide the context for the language and enable you to set the scene outside the teaching situation.

Do not teach words in isolation. This simply results in the student knowing lists of words but not being able to put them together meaningfully, e.g. NOT *'pen'?* but *'Have you got a pen?'*, NOT *'baby . . . sick . . . no come'* but *'My baby's sick. I can't come.'*

When you are introducing new vocabulary you can simply put it into a naming pattern: i.e. *'This is the library'*. *'This is a spanner'*, before using the words in the sentence you want to practise.

When a student has listened sufficiently then s/he must have the chance to repeat the language several times to get it right and to help her/him remember it. Encourage a student to imitate your pronunciation as far as possible. It helps to develop good habits from the beginning but remember that comprehensibility is the aim, not perfection. Encourage a student to imitate some of the non-verbal language as well, such as gesture and expression, as this is used differently in different cultures.

Target: To teach how to ask and say where places are in an area. To teach *'near, next to, opposite'*.

e.g. *'Where's the bank?'*. *'It's near the post office.'*

Known vocabulary: supermarket, station, school, bank, post office, garage, park (whatever is appropriate to the area). Where? questions already known.

Materials: simple map of the area showing places with pictures and labels.

1. **Check that the student knows the names of the places.**

   T. Look at the map. What's this?

   S. (It's) the school, etc.

2. **Demonstrate the new language**

   Use objects in the room to show the meaning of *'near, next to, opposite'*.

3. **Present the new words in the context you want to practise**

   T. Look at the map again. Listen.
   Where's the bank? It's next to the Post Office.
   Where's the supermarket? It's opposite the garage.
   Where's the park? It's near the school.

4. **Repetition**

   T. Now you answer after me.
   (Point to self) Where's the bank? *(Point to student)*
   (It's next to the Post Office.

   S. It's next to the Post Office, etc.

   T. Now you ask me. *(point to student)* Where's the garage?
   S. Where's the garage?
   T. It's opposite the supermarket, etc.

Note:

(i) The dialogue can be recorded on tape using two people to show that one person is asking and another answering. Sometimes beginner students repeat everything and do not realise you are asking a question. If you cannot tape it you can use a picture of two faces to illustrate conversation or use your hands like puppets to make the same point.

(ii) Make sure the student answers the questions using *'it's'* and does not repeat the name of the place being asked about. *'The park is near the school'* is a statement giving information. *'It's near the school'* is an answer to a question.

(iii) Contractions are used like *'It's'* to teach natural spoken English but a student needs to know the full form as well as s/he will hear it elsewhere and needs to use it when, for example, asking questions *'Is it . . .?'* Show the student like this: *Where is...?* (Indicate with your hands the two words coming together) *Where's? It is . . . It's*, etc.

Visuals

It is important to use visual materials to create context. You may find the items listed below useful.

- Photographs
- Pictures from magazines, brochures, catalogues, text books, picture dictionaries
- Real objects
- A calendar
- Tape measure
- Samples of materials/substances
- Timetables
- Maps, A-Z
- Packets and labels
- Leaflets and manuals
- Forms
- Tickets
- Bills
- Newspapers/magazines/TV Times/ Radio Times
- Advertisements
- Telephone book/Yellow Pages, a telephone.

Some of these resources may be available in other languages so that you can make use of a student's mother tongue. This gives value to a student's language and is useful for enhancing understanding.

Vocabulary development with intermediate and advanced students

Sometimes a particular goal of a student is to extend vocabulary. There is obviously no point in learning lists of words out of context but it can be useful to develop vocabulary on a theme or to show how related words are built up, e.g. *economics, economic, economy, economical, economist, uneconomical.*

At this level the meaning of new vocabulary can be shown by the language context not just a visual demonstration. Explanations and definitions can be used and the student should be encouraged to use a dictionary effectively.

Practice

1. Drills

Drills are to language learning what scales are to playing music. A drill is a set of sentences which follow the same pattern but with one or two words changed every time. Although the emphasis in language teaching is on communicative activities drills are useful in that they give repetitive practice to establish habits and encourage fluency. They are good for practising grammatical and functional patterns. There is a place for such activities just as there is for learning some things by heart (e.g. irregular verb forms).

How they can be used

(i) To practise new language as in the extract from a lesson described on page 49. They help a student get the order of words right, to remember to put all the little words in, to get the pronunciation right, to say the sentence fluently. As a student progresses you can build upon structures practised earlier, e.g. *'I'm looking for a shirt'* – *'I'm looking for a blue/long-sleeved/striped shirt.'* *'I liked science'* – *'I liked science because it was interesting/because we had a good teacher'*.

(ii) To give a student practice in saying something correctly and overlaying incorrect forms. For example: An intermediate student consistently says: *'I not go'* for *'I didn't go'*. You could make a list of things s/he did the day before and another list of things s/he does on other days and practise like this:

'Yesterday was a holiday. I stayed at home. I got up late. I went shopping. I took the children to the park. I didn't go to work/get up early/wash the vegetables/cut up the meat/pack the dishwasher/clean the kitchen.'

(iii) Always demonstrate clearly what a student has to do. Make sure that a student is not repeating something s/he does not understand. Make the drills as realistic as possible. Put them in a context and use visuals if appropriate.

(iv) Use them sparingly for a short time only.

Some examples

(i) Single word substitution **T.** Would you like a biscuit? **S.** *(Repeats)* **T.** Would you like a cake? **S.** *(Repeats)*	**T.** Would you like a chocolate? **S.** *(Repeats)* When you have demonstrated the drill you can simply *'cue'* the word to be changed. *'biscuit/cake/chocolate'*.

(ii) Progressive substitution
T. I had my car repaired last week
S. *(Repeats)*
T. He
S. He had his car repaired last week
T. washing machine
S. He had his washing machine repaired last week
T. on Friday
S. He had his washing machine repaired on Friday.

This helps students understand word order and structural changes.

(iii) Incremental
T. I typed
S. I typed
T. a letter
S. I typed a letter
T. to the manager
S. I typed a letter to the manager
T. this morning
S. I typed a letter to the manager this morning.

This type of drill helps fluency.

(iv) Contextual
Here the cue is a sentence which sparks off an appropriate response. For example:
T. What colour would you like?
S. I'd like a green/blue/red/brown one.
T. The car's dirty
S. Yes, it needs cleaning
T. The tyre's worn
S. Yes, it needs replacing
T. The brake is stiff
S. Yes, it needs adjusting.

2. Dialogues

Writing and selecting dialogues

In language teaching dialogues are scripted conversations between two or more people. They can show a student how language is used in a situation. However, in a situational dialogue there can be a wide range of grammatical features, expressions and functions. A dialogue prepared for listening practice and a dialogue for speaking practice are different. The first can contain some unknown language, hesitations and repetitions, while the second should only contain language a student already knows and needs to produce, or the language that you plan to teach a student. Therefore it is important to keep your dialogues fairly short and purposeful.

Here is an example:

> **Asking for directions:**
> A. Excuse me, could you tell me where the library is, please?
> B. Yes, go straight along this corridor, through those doors, up the stairs on your left to the second floor. When you get there turn right and the library is straight in front of you.
> A. Second floor, turn right. Thanks very much.
> B. You're welcome.

Suitable dialogues can also be selected from published materials. Check the content is appropriate and what structures and vocabulary are included.

Uses of dialogues

- to show a new language item in a context
- to practise a new item in a context
- to practise making appropriate responses
- to improve pronunciation and fluency
- to give a student confidence by having a clear script to work to.

How to present a dialogue

- It is best to record the dialogue on tape. You can then play it several times and it always sounds the same. It also gives a student the opportunity to hear a different voice. This is important in a 1:1 situation. If this is not possible you will have to read both parts yourself.
- Play the tape two or three times and check comprehension.
- You can either play the tape before drilling the important structures to set them in a context or drill the structures first.
- When you are both happy about the language in the dialogue, ask the student to take one of the parts. It is usual for a student to play the part s/he would in real life. So in the first example s/he could play either part. S/he might equally be in a situation where s/he needs to ask for or give directions. In the second, if s/he is likely to be a customer s/he would take part B. If s/he is involved in running a business s/he could take part A.
- Play the tape and stop it after each sentence the student is to speak. Ask her/him to repeat it.
- Then play the tape and stop it before each sentence and see if the student can say it. Alternatively you can each take your parts without using the tape at this stage.
- It is better if a student listens to and repeats the dialogue rather than reads it.

Reading can impede pronunciation and fluency. However a written transcription of the dialogue is useful for a student to keep for reference.

- If a student cannot read the use of the tape is even more important. S/he could keep a copy of the tape to listen to and practise at home.

Using the language

1. Role-play

What is role-play?

Drills and dialogues are both ways of practising language that are guided and controlled by a tutor. They give valuable support to a student in the learning process. However, the language is chosen by the tutor. There is no opportunity for the student to decide on the language to use or to have to think for her/himself and respond to something unexpected. They may also suggest that there is only one correct form of English for a given situation.

Role-play is a step nearer being able to use the language in a real situation outside the learning context. It is more flexible than dialogue, allowing for a variety of responses. It encourages students to listen to the other person and to make their own responses. You can draw language out of a student as you discuss what the possibilities are in a particular situation. You can explore degrees of formality, gestures, and tone. You can introduce variables such as dealing with unhelpful or hostile people. All this helps to build a student's confidence.

Role-play can be used in the same kinds of situation as scripted dialogue. The possibilities are endless: inviting a friend for coffee, taking something to be repaired and explaining the problem, phoning a college to ask for a crèche place, a job interview, asking the supervisor for a day off, etc.

Uses of role-play

- Role-play can be used at any level.
- It can be used as the culmination of controlled work such as drills and dialogues.
- It can be used to check learning.
- It can also be used as a starting point. In this case it is used diagnostically to find out how much a student knows and what aspects of language need further practice. For this reason it is a very useful technique with intermediate and advanced students.

How to conduct a role-play

Method A

The tutor sets up a functional framework for the role-play. This can give quite detailed guidance and in a sense is an intermediate stage between dialogue and free role-play.

For example:

Ladda has been practising taking orders in a restaurant. A role-play based on this situation could be structured as follows:

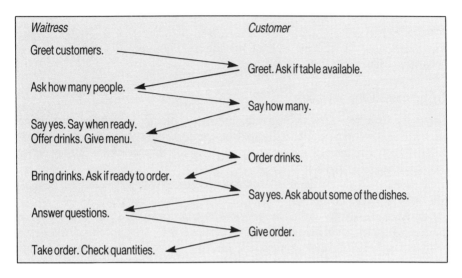

Note: This method requires a knowledge of functional terms. If you have used this language when teaching and the student understands the terms there is no problem. Sometimes, however, the functional description is harder than the language a student is expected to produce.

Go through the role-play step by step discussing with the student the best way of expressing the functions. Then act out the whole exchange. As with dialogues the student should play her/himself and the tutor the other part. If you record it on tape you can both listen and identify the strengths and weaknesses.

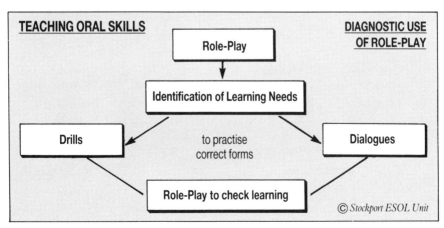

Method B

Set the scene in a more general way. For example:

*'You are the waitress and I am the customer. I haven't booked but you are not very busy.
You offer me drinks and take the order. I ask you some questions about the food and you try
to answer them.'*

You then act out the situation without much preparation, record it and then discuss
how it went afterwards.

2. Communication activities

These are materials devised to give a student practice in asking for and giving
information. Like role-play they give students the opportunity to formulate their own
questions and responses in a given situation. Again the emphasis is on fluency rather
than correctness of language.

These activities are usually used as pairwork exercises with a class but can be used
effectively in a 1:1 situation with you and a student forming the pair.

The materials are based on the information-gap principle. Person A has some
information which is not held by Person B. Person B must ask appropriate questions
to obtain this information. Sometimes only one person lacks information and
sometimes both people lack certain but different information which they must obtain
from each other. The information can be pictorial, diagrammatic or written. When the
missing information has been obtained it can be written or drawn on the worksheet.

Here is a simple example:

Some information is missing from your bus timetable. Ask questions to find out the information.
Answer your partner's questions.

A.

BUS TIMETABLE	
Service No. 192	
Frequency: Every..........minutes	
STOP	TIME
Hilltown	....
Red Lion	07.12
....	07.18
Hospital	....
Green Lane	07.30
Station	07.40

B.

BUS TIMETABLE	
Service No.	
Frequency: Every 30 minutes	
STOP	TIME
Hilltown	07.00
Red Lion	....
High Street	07.18
Hospital	07.25
....	07.30
Station	....

These beginnings might help you:

How often .... ?

What time .... ?

When .... ?

What number .... ?

What's the stop after .... ?

---

3. Monologue

Not all spoken language is interactive. Sometimes it is necessary to speak at greater length to somebody where little or no response is expected.

This often occurs in more formal situations such as on a college course, a training course or at work. A student may have to give instructions to a colleague, describe a process or present a talk to other students or trainees. If a student needs to be able to do any of these things, then choose a relevant topic and help the student plan the task.

This can be a guided activity with much of the content provided in the form of outline notes or information that the student reads or listens to and then retells.

It can be a free activity with the student providing the input. S/he can make notes on what s/he is going to say. However, it is better not to write out the whole thing as it then becomes more of a written exercise. The presentation can be recorded and discussed in the same way as a role-play.

4. Games

These add fun to a lesson, give lots of useful practice and can be used at all levels. There are many games which can fit in with particular types of language practice.

Kim's Game

Show a number of objects on a tray. Cover them and see how many the student can remember. Good for vocabulary.

Pelmanism

Place card sets face down. Pick up two cards at a time. If they match keep them, if not put them back. Good for matching words, pictures, words to pictures, opposites.

Snap

Similar to above but each player takes cards from a pack.

Adding items to a list

Each player has to remember all the items on a list and add a new item.

'I went shopping yesterday and I bought . . .'

'I'm going on holiday next week and I'm taking . . .'

Bingo

Use pictures and words instead of numbers. Past tenses can be practised by reading out the infinitives. The student has to find the past tense form on the card, e.g. *take/ took, write/wrote*.

Guessing games

Twenty questions to discover an object or well-known person.

Describe an object or person without naming them.

An example of materials using dialogue and role-play

Difficult neighbours

Role-play

Complaining to neighbours

The situation
You need to tell your neighbour about something that happens often and annoys you. Choose one of the following topics: loud music; dogs; cats; noisy children; smoke from a garden fire.

Before you start
Decide if you want to see your neighbour specially about this, or wait till you are in conversation with him.

Practise:
1. explaining the problem.
   What happens?
   How often does it happen?

2. starting the conversation
   introducing this topic into your conversation.
   Do you want to be polite or rude? Friendly or angry?
   How can you begin to tell your neighbour?

Role cards
A wants to complain to neighbour B.

A

1. ┌─────────────────────────────┐
   │ You already know B.   │ ←→
   │ He/she seems quite friendly.│
   └─────────────────────────────┘

2. ┌─────────────────────────────┐
   │ You have seen B, but he/she │ ←→
   │ never speaks to you.   │
   └─────────────────────────────┘

B

┌─────────────────────────────┐
│ You are a friendly   │
│ neighbour.   │
└─────────────────────────────┘

┌─────────────────────────────┐
│ You do not like to be too   │
│ friendly with neighbours.   │
│ Today you are in a   │
│ particularly bad mood.   │
└─────────────────────────────┘

Tape yourself and listen

A
Were you polite or rude?
Was B polite or rude?
Did you get what you wanted from B?
If not, was it your fault or B's?

B
Were you polite or rude?
Did you play a part similar to your own personality or different?

Grammar notes

Examples of grammar used in 'Talk about the pictures'

Basic language:
They play loud music.
The cat digs up the flowers.
The dog eats the cat's food.
The children climb over the fence.
People throw things over the wall.
When he uses his electric drill, the TV goes wrong.
When they have a party, the people downstairs can't sleep.

Difficult language:
They keep playing loud music.

People { sometimes / often / occasionally } throw things.

{ Every time / Whenever } he uses his drill . . .

Whenever the man in the flat downstairs uses his drill, the people in the flat above can't watch TV because the picture goes funny. When the people at number 10 play music, the woman next door gets angry.

Examples of grammar used in the dialogues
Sometimes our television goes wrong.
It doesn't happen all the time, just now and again.
He comes every day in front of my door. He dirties everywhere.
They play games outside my front door every day.
I think they don't do it. They do.

Suggestions for reading/writing practice
Writing a letter of complaint

Time after Time: Meryl Wilkins and Mike Baynham, National Extension College

Teaching Pronunciation

Some general points that can be made are:

- It is usual to combine pronunciation work with general speaking practice. This way it is closely related to the context a student is working on.
- Don't be a perfectionist. Only concentrate on the aspects that stop a student being understood.
- Become aware of the likely pronunciation difficulties for speakers of particular languages.
- When you and the student have identified the problems you want to work on, choose one problem at a time and work on it for about five minutes.
- Be aware of how you pronounce individual sounds, where you put the stress on words and in sentences and how you use intonation to express different meanings.
- Nobody can produce sounds they are unable to hear. The first step is listening and learning to discriminate similar sounds, to hear the stress and intonation.

How to teach pronunciation

1. Sounds.

If a sound does not exist in a student's language the student will substitute another similar sound. Sounds are significant only when in contrast with another. Therefore if a sound is mispronounced and becomes indistinguishable from another meaning is affected. It is useful, therefore, to practise sounds which give difficulty in minimal pairs such as *chip/cheap, day/they, shop/chop.*

(i) First the student needs to learn to discriminate between them.

It is hard to contextualise this kind of practice but always choose words that are known to a student. Write down the pairs of words. Say one word in each pair and ask the student to identify which one by pointing to it or circling it. If a student cannot read select words that can be shown pictorially and ask her/him to identify the picture.

For example:

To discriminate *p/b*

 pin/bin tap/tab pill/bill cap/cab park/bark pack/back

To discriminate *'teen'* and *'ty' in numbers.*

16/60   15/50   13/30

To discriminate *i/ee*

seat/sit   leave/live   feel/fill

59

To discriminate the sound of 'ed' in past
tense endings'

	t	d	id
arrived		✓	
visited			✓
watched	✓		

To discriminate e/a

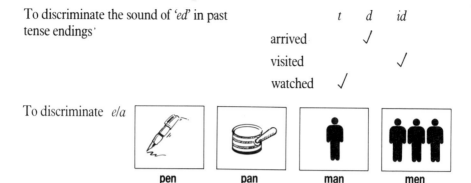

| pen | pan | man | men |

Another way is to say pairs of words and ask the student to say whether they are the same or different, e.g. tin/tin – S   thin/tin – D

You can say some words beginning or ending with the sounds you are practising and ask the student to tick the sound being used. With this exercise you do not have to keep to minimal pairs, e.g.

	sh	ch			
1	✓		Say	1	shop
2		✓		2	cheque
3		✓		3	chip
4	✓			4	shoe
5		✓		5	change

After listening to the sounds in individual words you can put them into sentences to listen to.

2. Stress

You can practise discrimination of stress patterns by saying words or sentences and asking a student to underline the stressed syllable. Then ask her/him to try saying it in the same way. You can beat the rhythm to make it more emphatic. Where there is significant stress ask the student what meaning is expressed by it, e.g. *Thach* passed his exam. (but Omer didn't).

3. Intonation

Similarly ask a student first to listen and say whether your voice is going up or down and then to try and imitate it.

With all pronunciation work a cassette recorder is invaluable. You can play the model over and over again and it will always sound the same. You can record a student and s/he can compare her/his pronunciation with the model.

Working independently

All the activities described in this chapter are intended to be done by a student and tutor working together. This is not always possible in open learning centres. In any case it is important to encourage all students towards being independent in their learning. You do not have to be working with a student all the time.

Some materials can be adapted for use by students working on their own. The materials need clear instructions, in English or the mother tongue, written or taped. It is also useful if answers are provided so students can check their own work.

A student can then listen to materials recorded on cassette and follow instructions to record her/his own responses. S/he can listen to and repeat drills, dialogues and pronunciation exercises.

It may also be possible for a group of students who are at approximately the same level to get together to practise dialogues and role-play situations.

Encourage a student to use her/his mother tongue in a constructive way. S/he can keep a personal dictionary to write down useful words and phrases together with the mother tongue equivalent. S/he might find it helpful to transcribe English words into the mother tongue sound system as a guide to pronunciation.

Further reading

Active Listening, R.R. Jordan, Collins 1984 EFL (for discrimination of sounds, etc.)

At Home in Britain, K. Harding et al. National Extension College 1982. Packs for beginner and elementary students ESOL

English for Driving, V. Barr and C. Fletcher, National Extension College 1984. Multi-lingual.

LDA Learning Development Aids. Useful sets of picture cards.

A New Start, P. Furnborough, S. Cowgill, H. Greaves, K. Sapin, Heinemann 1980. For beginners. ESOL. Out of print.

Open Learning and ESOL, Liz Voss, ALBSU 1991.

Speak for Yourself, D. Gubbay and S. Cowgill, BBC 1980. Out of Print. For intermediates. Good for role-play.

Talkback, Coventry Communication Education Project. Packs on everyday topics.

Teaching English Pronunciation: Tree or Three? (Elementary) 1982, *Ship or Sheep?* (Intermediate) 1981, Ann Baker, Cambridge University Press, EFL.

Telephoning in English, Naterop and Revell, Cambridge University Press 1987. Adv. EFL.

Time after Time, Meryl Wilkins and Mike Baynham, National Extension College 1986. Intermediate. Tense usage in useful contexts, but poor quality recordings. ESOL.

Topics and Skills in English, V. Barr and C. Fletcher, Hodder and Stoughton 1983. Good for intermediate students. ESOL.

Vocabulary Builders 1&2, Bernard Seal, Longham 1988. EFL.

There are many EFL materials which, if selected carefully for appropriateness, can be used with ESOL students. Only a few are mentioned above.

7 | Developing Reading and Writing Skills – 1

Planning

Chapter 2 examined how to start planning a learning programme with a student. The first step was to identify long and short term goals and break these down into the skills needed. This chapter looks at reading and writing skills, approaches to teaching these skills to beginner and elementary students and the kinds of material that can be used.

1. Needs

The five students featured in Chapter 1 exemplify a considerable range of reading and writing goals.

Sakeena: Knowing the sounds of letters, recognising relevant words, names and address, children's names, social sight, key words. Letter formation, filling in a simple form.

Thach: Reading letters and bills, job adverts, maps, safety instructions at work, car manuals. Writing cheques/giro, filling in application forms, writing letters.

Yasmin: Reading newspapers, letters, textbooks, children's books, writing letters, filling in application forms, writing a CV, making notes, writing essays and assignments.

Omer: Reading job adverts, training information, newspapers. Writing CV, application forms, letters and eventually articles.

Ladda: Reading signs and labels, letters, cleaning instructions, a menu, safety instructions. Filling in a time-sheet, filling in forms, writing a cheque.

2. What sort of skills are needed to achieve these goals?

Basic reading skills include:

- directing reading from left to right
- knowing the names and the sounds of letters
- knowing sound/spelling relationships
- distinguishing upper and lower case letters
- recognising 'key' words, e.g. *this, is, has, the*
- recognising where a word or sentence ends

- knowing how to blend sounds together
- understanding as well as working out what a word is (decoding)
- using context.

More advanced reading skills include:
- reading words as groups rather than word by word
- skimming and scanning
- predicting and using context to identify a word (context cueing)
- making analogies
- knowing how texts are structured
- understanding both surface meaning and inferences.

Basic writing skills include:
- holding a pen/pencil correctly
- moving from left to right
- forming letters correctly both upper and lower case
- spacing words.

More advanced skills include:
- knowing when to use upper and lower case letters
- punctuation
- spelling
- paragraphing
- layout
- grammar
- appropriate style.

3. Prior learning

The next step is to look at a student's previous learning experience and see which of these skills the student has already acquired in her/his mother tongue and in English. Some skills may be transferable from the first language to English but other factors may hinder the process of reading and writing in English.

The relevant factors when considering first language literacy are:
- the system and direction of writing in the first language
- the general level of education in country of origin
- the level of literacy in the first language
- the use of literacy in the first language
- differences between the first language and English, e.g. in sounds and in structure.

An additional factor is whether the student has learnt to speak, read or write any other languages.

Factors connected with the student's experience of English are:

- Educational experience in Britain
- Length of stay and experience of life in Britain
- Oral competence in English
- Gap in competence between listening, speaking, reading and writing skills.

For example: **Ladda** and **Yasmin** both used a different script in their first language but **Yasmin** was also highly literate in English. **Ladda** has transferable skills but has had to learn a new script.

Sakeena, on the other hand, did not have the opportunity to go to school in Pakistan. She is not literate in either Urdu or English. She has to learn both the concept and the basic skills of literacy.

Other students, who can read and write in Urdu or Arabic but are total beginners in English, have conceptual skills to transfer to English but nevertheless have to learn a totally new script and to direct their reading from right to left.

Thach and **Omer** are both familiar with the Roman script but have to learn new sound values for the letters. **Thach's** difficulties with pronunciation will affect his ability to spell. **Omer** was a beginner in English in all skills so his lack of knowledge of grammar and vocabulary will be reflected in his literacy skills. However, his experience of learning French, his level of education and his lack of exposure to spoken English could mean that his reading level moves ahead faster than his spoken English.

4. Assessing reading and writing skills

In Chapter 2 some suggestions were made on suitable tasks for assessing reading and writing skills in English. For initial assessment of reading it is better to talk through the text you have selected rather than give written exercises. In this way you can adapt your approach to the individual, asking questions to check understanding, asking a student to select bits of information and maybe read some of the text aloud. See if a student can tackle an unfamiliar word or guess at its meaning. In this way you can assess a student's ability in some of the skills identified above. When assessing writing you can observe how s/he holds the pen, forms the letters and how fluently s/he writes, as well as analysing the result in terms of grammar, spelling, punctuation, etc.

5. What materials to use

When learning a language, listening and speaking come before reading and writing. Reading materials must, therefore, be within a student's spoken competence. This is particularly true in the early stages. Only when a student is a reasonably confident reader should new words be introduced through the written text. However, even at an advanced stage there should not be too high a proportion of unknown words. It is also important that reading is not an isolated activity but is closely related to and integrated with listening and speaking practice.

Reading materials can be:

Texts based on spoken language practice. These could be a written dialogue or a paragraph or some sentences which reflect the structures or functions being taught. These are specially written texts designed to be within the learner's oral competence. You can write them yourself or choose appropriate texts from a course book. They are useful in reinforcing the spoken language. However, if a student's reading competence is far behind her/his spoken competence you will have to select a simple sentence within her/his capabilities. It is not always necessary to be able to read what is spoken and for beginner readers it may be better to concentrate on reading which relates to the spoken context but is at the right level.

Example: Reading from a substitution table can reinforce oral practice.

What do you like doing? / What does he/she like doing?		
I We	like	cooking swimming
Wendy My son	likes	driving watching TV

Texts based on a student's language experience. The tutor writes a text based on a student's own words when talking about experiences and opinions. This ensures that the language is within a student's oral competence and that the subject matter is of interest. This could lead to the development of a personal reading book.

You agree with the student the sentences to be written down bearing in mind the level of competence in reading. It is also important with a language student that any errors in the spoken language are discussed and corrected before the sentences are written down. There is no point in a student reinforcing errors by reading them. (The language experience approach is widely used in adult literacy classes).

Graded readers. These are books at different levels written specially for learners. The language at each level is controlled with regard to structure and vocabulary so it can match the spoken competence of a student. There is usually plenty of repetition to help a student remember words. Sometimes the language may be rather stilted and unnatural and sometimes the stories may not be very interesting. However, reading a story can give enjoyment and a sense of achievement. ESOL students who are fluent speakers do not need such tight control over structure and vocabulary.

Authentic texts. These are real texts appropriate for the areas selected by a student: e.g.

signs, labels, advertisements, letters, articles, materials and books from a college or training course. It is important to try to select materials at a suitable level. Signs and notices, even though short, can use difficult vocabulary and structures.

Teaching reading to beginners

There are a number of approaches used to teach reading to beginners who are native speakers of English. Three of the commonly used ones are:

1. whole word recognition   2. context   3. phonics

It is useful to consider how effective and appropriate they might be with beginner readers who are speakers of other languages bearing in mind the factors listed at the beginning of this chapter.

1. Whole word recognition

What is it?

This approach aims at meaningful reading by a student learning to recognise a known word as a whole. The word is identified for the student by someone reading it or by a picture. The student looks at the word and says it. By constant repetition the student learns to recognise the word as an entity. It is similar to a Chinese speaker learning to recognise Chinese characters. The skills of visual discrimination and memory are involved in identifying the word. Memory is an essential element in learning to read whatever approach is used.

Its use with ESOL students

This approach is useful for ESOL students, especially beginners such as **Sakeena,** who are not literate in the mother tongue and do not have transferable skills.

For those who can read in their mother tongue, whatever the script, it provides a useful starting point but they will soon want to develop strategies for reading independently. Students like **Ladda** will want to relate symbols with sounds in the same way as she can in Thai. Students like **Omer,** who already know the Roman script, would be able to have a go at reading English right from the beginning, but would not be sure how to pronounce words. They may find the approach useful as they can listen to the sounds of a word and begin to build up a picture of the sound/ spelling relationship in English. They, too, will want to move on rapidly to acquire strategies for independent reading and will be able to transfer some of those strategies from their mother tongue experience.

How to use the whole word method
- Select the words/sentences to be read.

- If you are writing them, write clearly with good spacing. Line breaking can be helpful, e.g.

- Present the words in context, e.g. with background or accompanying pictures, in a sentence, on a form.

- Read aloud to the student pointing to the words.

- Ask the student to read with you.

- Encourage the student to read alone. Help out when there is difficulty.

- Ask the student to pick out individual words. Start with any already known.

- Do not present too many new words at a time.

- In the early stages avoid teaching words that look similar at the same time.

- Remember that a student will need to see the word many times before instant recognition is achieved.

- Check understanding.

- Remember that a student may memorise words in a particular context or on a particular page and not be able to read them in another context.

- You can record the text (individual words to a whole reader) for a student to listen to and follow on her/his own. This is essential in open learning and useful for any student.

2. Using Context and Predicting

What does this mean?

This approach also aims at identifying whole words. It encourages a student to concentrate on the meaning of a whole sentence or text and to use the context of a word or sentence to predict or guess what a word is. The visual context (illustrations, surroundings) and a student's expectations of what a text is about are also important. At this level context is being used to read a word that is within a student's spoken competence.

Using context with ESOL students

This technique can be used to some extent at all levels of reading but is most useful for students with a good command of spoken English. ESOL students have more difficulty than first language speakers in using verbal context because their knowledge of structure and vocabulary may not be enough to be able to predict with any accuracy. Providing a visual context is helpful to all students.

67

However, at beginner and elementary level, a student is only expected to read what s/he can speak. Therefore, if a student reads a text based on spoken language practice, the vocabulary and topic will be familiar and s/he will be able to use this knowledge to predict words not read before. If the text is a well-known story or on a topic a student knows at lot about then again expectation or knowledge of what comes next will help the student read the text.

e.g.   She went to the shop to *buy* some eggs.

You can pay by *cheque* or credit card.

A student who is unsure about 'buy' or 'cheque' could guess the words from the context, especially if s/he could also recognise the first sound 'b' or 'ch'.

This approach encourages students to use their own knowledge and experience and to become more independent when reading. ESOL students, like **Omer**, who can read well in the mother tongue but are beginners in English, will already use this skill and will be able to apply it to English within the limitations of their spoken competence.

How to use context

- Prepare the student for the text before s/he starts to read by introducing it and talking about it.

- Encourage the student to look through the whole text first to get an idea of what it is about.

- Show the student how to use the layout, headlines, illustrations to help understanding.

- If there is a word or phrase a student cannot read encourage her/him to read the whole sentence, to look back at the previous sentence and to look forward to the next sentence.

A useful technique for developing the use of context is gap-filling. It is helpful, especially at beginner and elementary levels, to provide the missing words in random order to choose from or to give a choice of words for each gap of which only one is correct.

It is important to check that a student has predicted a word correctly. Sometimes it is not possible to guess a word from its context and other reading strategies have to be used.

3. Phonics

What are phonics?

A phonic approach to teaching reading is based on the relationship between a letter or a group of letters of the alphabet and a particular sound. A student may be able to sound out the letters in a word, blend them together and read the word, e.g.

s–a–t = sat, ch–a–t = chat.

There are then many combinations of vowels and consonants which relate to particular sounds and rules governing the pronunciation of letters in certain combinations, e.g. The two sounds of 'g' in the word 'garage'.

Using phonics with ESOL students

Phonics can help a student begin to tackle reading words independently. If a word is known to a student, then one or two phonic clues may be enough to identify the word combined with the use of context.

It is usual to begin with the regular letter/sounds which match the phonic alphabet, e.g. many consonant sounds at the beginning and end of words, followed by short vowel sounds in the middle of words such as 'man', 'pen'. Then other combinations can be introduced gradually.

Some points to bear in mind are:

- the most commonly used words in English (the 'key' words) are among the most irregular.

- English is not phonetically regular therefore there are a number of variations and exceptions to learn. This can be frustrating for all students whether they are first language speakers or speakers of other languages. ESOL students whose mother tongue is phonetically regular (i.e. the same letters always have the same sound) will approach the relationship between spelling and sound on the basis of previous learning and may find the irregularities particularly annoying.

- Reading schemes based on phonics often involve reading lists of phonetically similar words which may be unfamiliar to the student and not very useful to know,

  e.g. *moon, hoop, boon, boom*.

  Sentences based on such words can be unnatural and not the sort of language a student needs to learn.

- Phonics can lead to single letter analysis which hinders fluency and the use of context. In the effort to work out what a word is the meaning can be lost. In addition learning a lot of rules creates a big memory load.

- Some sounds may not exist in a student's mother tongue. However, this effects listening comprehension and spelling more than reading. A student can see that '*ship*' and '*chip*' are different words and have a different meaning even if s/he cannot pronounce them differently.

- Students like **Thach** and **Omer** will only need to concentrate on the differences between their first language and English – the letters that have different sound values, letter/sounds that do not exist in the mother tongue, different letter/sound combinations.

How to use phonics

- Use phonics when a student has built up recognition by the whole word method of a reasonably sized bank of words.

- Make sure a student who is used to a different writing system can discriminate individual letters and can relate upper and lower case letters. This can be done by matching exercises:

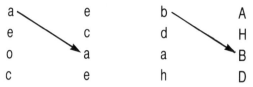

- Make sure a student knows the difference between the names (for spelling) and the sounds of the letters. It can help to make a picture dictionary focussing on the sound at the beginning of the word.
- Practise identifying the letters/letter groups in texts in different writing and print.
- Always use words within a student's spoken vocabulary and preferably ones the student can already read by sight.
- Group these words according to a particular letter or letter group/sound relationship. Group according to first, middle, or final sounds, e.g.

number	man	shop
nationality	hand	fish
name	back	shoe

- As a student progresses you can introduce common sequences:

  ee, ea, ou, or, er, ai, st, ing, able, tion, ight, etc.

  This helps a student move from looking at individual letters to the syllable. It is important here to show that the same spelling can have different sounds and group the words accordingly.

  head/bread but *meat/eat*

- Encourage a student to compare a new word with words already known where there are similarities.
- Show a student how to break longer words into syllables – na/tion/al/i/ty
- Teach some useful rules, e.g. Final 'e' lengthens the previous vowel sound – *name, made, ice.*

In conclusion it can be said that none of these approaches is ideal on its own and in many ways they complement each other. It is best to use a combined approach taking into account a student's preferences and previous learning and experience.

Reading aloud

Reading aloud is necessary with beginners so that you can listen to, check, and help them with their reading. However, it is important to encourage a student towards silent reading as soon as possible. If you feel fairly sure a student can cope with most of a text, it is often better to ask the student to read it to her/himself first. You can then check understanding and the ability to say and pronounce the words in the text by asking oral questions. You can spot check particular words and talk about any words that presented difficulties.

Using a dictionary

Teach a student from the very early stages to use a dictionary. This could be a bi-lingual dictionary or an English-English dictionary. There are useful bi-lingual picture dictionaries and learner's dictionaries at all levels.

Teaching basic writing skills

In the sequence of skills, writing follows reading. Students should only write what they can say, understand and read. Writing can reinforce speaking and reading practice especially if all the skills are approximately at the same level.

However, writing is by far the most difficult skill. Like speaking it is productive but tends to get less practice than speaking. It is less essential, people can manage without it or get someone else to do it.

As we saw at the beginning of the chapter it involves a lot of skills; the mechanics of writing, knowing the language to use (grammar mistakes become much more obvious when written down), spelling and punctuation. There may be a considerable gap between a student's level of speaking and reading and between the level of reading and writing.

1. Teaching Handwriting

Students who are not able to read or write in the mother tongue or whose mother tongue uses a different script will need to learn the mechanics of writing.

- A student who has not written before will need to be shown how to sit and how to hold a pen/pencil.
- Writing patterns help a student get used to some of the shapes in the Roman Script and the left to right movement.

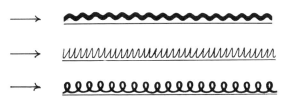

- Teach a student to form the letters correctly both upper and lower case using a clear simple print. Many students are familiar with capital letters and yet for reading and most writing tasks lower case are more important.

- Teach the relationship of the letters to the line.

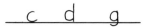

- Teach the student how to form numbers.

- Give plenty of practice. Tracing or overwriting is helpful as well as copying.

My name is Sakeena

- There is no need to teach a student to write all the letters at once. You can start with those that s/he needs to write for her/his name, etc.

2. Writing for communication purposes

Students with basic writing skills may have limited goals for writing, such as being able to fill in a simple form or write a note. Writing their name and address, telephone number and date of birth are essential skills for everyday life.

As a student gains confidence with writing or if a student can already use the Roman script you need to give plenty of guided practice in writing. This means that a student is not expected to write freely but follows a model or makes choices thus avoiding grammatical or spelling pitfalls. These techniques help to give a student confidence and reinforce correct language.

As well as developing writing skills for specific goals, written exercises can give useful reinforcement to spoken language practice and reading activities.

It is also useful to show the relationship between the spoken language and the written language. For example:

'Can I see the headteacher about Wendy, please?'

Dear Mrs Brown,
I would like to make an appointment to see you about my daughter, Wendy ...

3. Guided writing activities

- Copying: name and address, messages and simple letters, sentences giving personal information, sentences written for reading practice, e.g. language experience.

- Selecting and copying sentences from a substitution table or from a model with multiple choice options.

- Writing jumbled words/sentences in the correct order.

- Gap filling, choosing words from a selection in random order.

- Writing a parallel paragraph based on a model substituting different information.

- It can be helpful for some students if instructions for an exercise and maybe some key words can be written in the first language. Others do not want this kind of support and prefer to make their own decisions about what to put into the mother tongue.

- It can also be useful at times for a student to make notes in the mother tongue of what s/he wants to write in English. However, it is better for a student to use language and structures s/he knows in English rather than try to translate langauge from the mother tongue which is far in advance of the level of competence in English.

An example of a substitution table for writing a note.

I He She My son My daughter	can't	come go	to	work school class the meeting	tomorrow tonight on Friday

Further reading

An Introduction to Literacy Teaching (New Edition), Rose Gittins, ALBSU 1992.

Bilingual Toolkit, L. Oliphant et al, National Extension College 1988.

ESL/Literacy, Monica Turner – handbook for tutors ALBSU 1985. Out of print.

Literacy and Second Language Students, Anne Slater, ALBSU Newsletter No 16.

Literacy work with bi-lingual students, Monica Turner, ALBSU 1985. Out of print.

Start by Writing (Handwriting book), Jon Naunton, Longman EFL.

The Starter Pack, ALBSU 1991. (Basic Skills).

Teaching literacy to bi-lingual adults, handbook and readers; Ethnic Minorities Language Services, Newcastle Education Committee 1991.

Dictionaries
Oxford Elementary Dictionary
Oxford Picture Dictionaries (bi-lingual).

8 | Developing Reading and Writing Skills – 2

This chapter looks at developing reading and writing skills at an intermediate to advanced level, identifying and correcting errors, and spelling.

Integrated language work in the four language skills can be done when a student can use all the skills at more or less the same level, even if that level is basic or elementary. When there is a gap, for example, between spoken skills and literacy skills then work can be done on the same topic but not at the same level. They are not fully integrated.

At intermediate level it should be possible to carry out integrated activities, e.g. listening and note-taking, discussing then writing on a topic, phoning about a problem and following up the phone call with a formal letter, etc. It also means that the sequence listening, speaking, reading, writing need not always be followed. Reading an article can be the stimulus for discussion. A story can be read and retold orally. New vocabulary can be learnt from written contexts.

Reading skills

1. Silent reading

At this stage fast silent reading should be encouraged. Reading aloud is necessary with beginners to check accuracy and pronunciation but it leads to slow word by word reading. You only need to read aloud when reading to someone else, like a child. You may find that some students have had little experience of silent reading and tend to mouth the words as they read. Fluency in reading can be improved by showing a student how to read in phrases or word groups, e.g.

> Complete the application form/in black ink/and return/to the Personnel Officer/as soon as possible.

2. Understanding

A student who has become proficient at the decoding process may be able to read a text fluently without being able to understand it. It may be that the text is too full of unknown words and is therefore too difficult but it may be that the student finds it difficult to get meaning from the written word and needs guidance in developing understanding.

The purpose of reading

At the beginning of Chapter 7 some of the types of reading students may need to do were identified. What, in more detail, does this entail?

If **Thach** has to read a car manual he has to cope with technical language. He also has to follow precise instructions. Scientific and technical language often uses the passive, e.g.

> After two years the cooling system must be flushed out and the coolant replaced.

In reading a newspaper article **Omer** may not need to read everything with such care and may only need to take in the main points. He will have to cope with different styles and with idiomatic and colloquial language. He may have to differentiate fact from opinion.

In reading books for her course **Yasmin** may have to deal with a more formal style, skim to get the gist and select the parts that require more thorough study. Again she will need to distinguish fact from opinion. She will have to select the main points for note-taking and summarising.

Developing understanding

You need to set some tasks to develop a student's reading skills and understanding of a text. Pre-reading questions can give a focus to the reading. Encourage a student to look at layout, illustrations, headings, titles and contents pages to predict what a text or book is about. Suggest the student reads through the whole text before starting on the tasks.

Although a student is encouraged to try using context to work out the meaning of new words it is nevertheless very important for a student to develop good dictionary skills. It is a good idea to practise using an English/English dictionary as well as a bilingual dictionary. A good learner's dictionary gives examples and show the usage of words. Students can also use dictionaries to find out how a word is pronounced.

There are many techniques for developing understanding such as open and multiple choice questions, true/false statements, matching activities, sequencing, summarising, information transfer, Cloze and other gap filling exercises.

Extending Reading Skills (ALBSU) is a useful handbook if you want ideas on how to extend your students' reading.

Writing skills

1. Handwriting

If a student still uses print you could encourage her/him to develop a cursive (joined up) writing style. This will help the student write more quickly and fluently. On the other hand a student may write quickly but untidily. Handwriting practice in either case is useful.

2. Free writing

In Chapter 7 some ideas for guided writing were presented. At intermediate level a student needs to be able to write independently, but it is a big jump from guided to free writing.

You can help a student with written work by careful preparation. Whether the task is a letter, an assignment for a training or college course or a piece of creative writing, the procedure is the same.

(a) Clarify the purpose of the letter, the meaning of the title of the assignment.

(b) Discuss what should go in it. The student can jot down ideas in English or the mother tongue.

(c) Check the student has got all the necessary information.

(d) Plan the framework, the sequence of ideas.

(e) Discuss the language involved. What functions, grammar, style need to be used? For example: Letter – asking for information, complaining, requesting actions. Assignment – describing, narrating, comparing, discussing issues. Who is the reader? Should the style be formal or informal?

(f) The student writes a draft.

(g) Encourage the student to proof-read looking for grammatical errors, checking spelling and punctuation.

(h) You read it and draw attention to any remaining errors. Discuss layout and paragraphing.

Look at these titles and choose the functions and tenses from the lists that you would use in each piece of writing. You may use more than one for each.

Title	Functions	Tenses
• The good and bad effects of TV on children.		
• Select and describe a toy suitable for a three year old.		
• How to make a paper lantern.		
• My childhood.		

Functions: Describing your experiences, describing an object, giving opinions, comparing and contrasting, giving reasons, giving instructions.

Tenses: Present simple, past simple, used to, imperative, models (should/ought to/must, etc.)

(Based on Self Access Worksheets, National Extension College)

(i) The student corrects and writes the final version.

To help a student like **Yasmin** become aware of the functions and tenses required for different types of writing you could do an exercise like the one at the bottom of the previous page.

3. Identifying writing needs

Just as you identified a student's language needs by listening to her/his spoken English so you should identify needs based on a student's writing.

(a) What to look out for:

(i) Overall impression: is the communication successful?

(ii) Organisation: of ideas, of sentences and paragraphs.

(iii) Grammar: tenses, articles, plurals, etc.

(iv) Word Order

(v) Punctuation

(vi) Spelling

(vii) Vocabulary

(viii) Style

(ix) Handwriting

Here is an example of a student's writing with some comments.

I finest the school days, otter that I am going to went to East Affica. Hero Kericho. tea co. I leave three month's otter that I start to work am leath operet masin. my brother teach me How to work and operet masin otter I year and 6 th month I am going to other towen kisumu I work there nyanza oil malls and rice mills I am work Fefeen year's when I am came here 1975 in London. I got a job ewellders I work five month's in London I leave t got a house for live So. I am went to Bradford there I got a house but k I hav't gut job I was ill three years

This student is from East Africa. He speaks and writes Gujerati. He describes his work experience and some of the difficulties he has had in getting work in Britain.

Comments

(i) *Overall impression:* Successful; although there are errors there is no real difficulty in understanding the sequence of events described.

Unsuccessful; some re-reading necessary to sort out sentences.

(ii) *Organisation:* Successful; chronological order; linking words like 'after that', 'and', 'but', 'so'.

Unsuccessful; sentence division and paragraphs.

(iii) *Grammar:* Successful; plurals mainly correct; prepositions – 'to East Africa', 'to Bradford', one or two correct verb forms.

Unsuccessful; use of past tense – uses present tense 'I start', 'I work' or inserts 'am', e.g. 'I am work'. Some prepositions 'in London' omission of '(at)' 'Nyanza oil mills'.

(iv) *Word order:* Mainly correct.

(v) *Punctuation:* Successful; capital letters for names of places.

Unsuccessful; lack of capitals and full-stops to show sentence division. Wrong use of 's.

(vi) *Spelling:* Mainly successful; a few words spelt as pronounced – 'finest', 'operet', 'masin'.

(vii) *Vocabulary:* Adequate but a bit repetitive.

(viii) *Style:* Not applicable.

(ix) *Handwriting:* Neat and legible. 'a', 'o', 'u' not always clearly distinguished. Would flow better if joined.

(b) Follow up exercises

When you have done such an analysis you need to encourage the student by pointing out the successful parts. Then decide with the student what areas are the most important to concentrate on.

In this case the tutor and student decided to work on simple past tense forms and sentence division.

(c) Causes of errors

It is useful to consider why a student makes certain mistakes. They may be caused by mother tongue influence or a partially learnt rule. A student who has acquired the language informally may not have heard certain features such as the 'ed' past tense ending or the ' 'm' in 'I'm going' and will not be aware of these differences. Sometimes false analogies are made. In the previous example the student may never have heard the past tense ending 'ed'. He may insert 'am' on analogy with 'I am going'.

He has learnt ' 's' for possession and extended the rule to plural –s as well.
He pronounces the 'sh' sound as 's' which affects his spelling.
Gujerati does not have capital letters so making a distinction between the upper and lower case has to be learnt.

(d) Correcting a student's writing work

Earlier in this chapter the importance of helping a student become aware of language and of proof-reading written work for mistakes was mentioned. However s/he can only correct things s/he knows about.

There are different opinions about the extent to which written work should be corrected. Should every mistake or only the most important mistakes be corrected? The answer perhaps depends on the level of the student, the number of errors and the purpose of the writing.

If an advanced student makes a few mistakes it would seem sensible to point them all out. On the other hand, if there are a lot of mistakes, it would be disheartening to deal with them all.

Rather than write in corrected forms it is better to underline the errors and see if the student can correct any of the mistakes. Students often can when the mistake is pointed out to them.

You can indicate the kind of error by using a code, e.g. P = punctuation, WO = word order, Sp = spelling, G = grammar, Voc. = vocabulary (you will need to teach a student what you mean by these terms).

If a student cannot correct the mistake give an example or a simple explanation to help.

Ask the student to write down the corrected words or sentences. This reinforces the correct forms and helps the student remember them another time.

Devise some exercises on the priority areas as follow up work.

Here is an example of a piece of corrected writing: a student describes his work in Pakistan.

4. Spelling

In spelling a student has to try to relate the sound of a word to a written form. Therefore a student's pronunciation as a result of sound differences between the mother tongue and English may lead to difficulties. In addition unstressed sounds are not easily heard and may be omitted.

Just as with learning to read, students whose first language is written phonetically may find the irregularities and variations of English spelling puzzling and irritating.

However, there are some useful rules and an awareness of these and common letter groups can help a student tackle words s/he is not sure of.

It is important that words used for spelling activities, like those used in phonic exercises, should be known to a student. Exercises for native English speakers may use uncommon words because they fit into a particular pattern.

ESOL students may not have the same difficulties as some native English speakers. For example, the confusion between *where* and *wear*, *here* and *hear* may not occur because the words were learnt according to their meaning and the appropriate spelling associated with them. They are not connected in the student's mind.

There are a variety of strategies for remembering spelling.

(a) Look/cover/write/check. This procedure helps imprint the spelling on the memory.

(b) Memorising a difficult spelling by:

  – a saying or a rhyme, e.g. 'i' before 'e' except after 'c'.

  – saying a word as it is spelled, e.g. Wed/nes/day.

(c) Find and match helps recognition of what looks right or wrong.

	A	B	C	D
HEIGHT	heigt	height	heigth	hieght

(d) Complete the word. This can focus on particular parts of the word or each letter in turn, e.g. Thursday/Th–rsday/T–ursday.

(e) Group words with the same sound and spelling, i.e. station/nation/relation.

(f) See if a student can deduce the rule.

took	week	back	book	sock	clock

(g) Show the range of possible spellings for a sound.

  e.g. The long sound i: s<u>ee</u>, <u>ea</u>t, thi<u>e</u>f, th<u>e</u>s<u>e</u>

  The 'sh' sound in word endings sta<u>ti</u>on, exten<u>si</u>on, spe<u>ci</u>al

(h) Word jigsaws

(i) Word building:

- being aware of prefixes and suffixes;

    un–   im–   dis–   –ful   –able   –ment

- related words help especially where there are sound changes

    relative/relation   revision/revise

5. Other writing activities

(a) Dictation

This may seem an old-fashioned exercise but it can give useful practise in relating the sounds and structure of the spoken language to the spelling and punctuation needed for the written. It should be based on language already familiar to a student.

(b) Note-taking

This is an important skill for a student like **Yasmin**. Notes can be taken from a book or a talk or lecture. Listening and note-taking is likely to be the more difficult. As with dictation a student has to relate the spoken language to the written but also select and organise the information.

A student may find it helpful to take some notes in the mother tongue even though it means doing an instant translation.

(c) Creative writing

These chapters have concentrated on practical writing needs – the essentials. These will be all many students can cope with or want to do. Some students, however, may enjoy trying their hand at creative writing. Quite often ideas for this may come out of a discussion topic or a reading text. Just as with any other sort of writing, talk about the topic first to get the ideas going. If a student finds it easier to talk than write you could record her/his ideas and then help her/him to write them down.

Some possible themes and starting points are: customs and traditions, memories, people, feelings, TV programmes, a newspaper article, pictures/cartoons, a prompt sheet of opinions, an opening sentence.

6. Word processors and computers

If these are available some students may enjoy and find it useful to develop writing skills using a word processor. This frees students from the mechanics of handwriting, enables them to correct and change what they have written easily and at the same time teaches a new and useful skill. Language activities and spelling games on computer may seem more fun than paper and pencil ones.

See Chapter 10 for more details on using computers and wordprocessors.

Further reading

Developing Reading Skills, F. Grellet, Cambridge University Press 1981 (for teachers).

Extending Reading Skills, ALBSU 1987, Basic Skills

Help Yourself to English, a self-study for ESOL students with good reading skills who want to improve their grammatical and functional accuracy. Books 1 and 2: Social context – elementary to intermediate; Books 3 and 4: Vocational context – intermediate; Book 5: Academic context – up to pre-GCSE level. Photocopiable. R. Leach, E. Knight, J. Johnson, National Extension College 1989.

Language Guidelines: Developing reading, writing and oral skills across the curriculum, Alistair Smith, Hodder and Stoughton 1990.

Language Power: Communication skills for a multi-racial society, Bob Matthews, National Extension College 1988. Photocopiable. ESOL.

Reading for Information, 5 books. Lancashire Industrial Language Training Unit. ESOL (for work and training situation).

Self Access Worksheets Books 1 and 2, Erica Buckmaster. Photocopiable. National Extension College 1986. Basic Skills.

Writing a CV, R. Leach, National Extension College 1989.

Grammar

English Grammar in Use (with answers), R. Murphy, Cambridge University Press 1985, EFL Intermediate.

Essential Grammar in Use (with answers), R. Murphy, Cambridge University Press 1990, EFL Elementary.

Grammar Practice Activities: a practical guide for teachers, Penny Ur, Cambridge University press, EFL.

Oxford Practice Grammar (with answers), John Eastwood, Oxford University Press 1992.

Self Access Grammar, Erica Buckmaster, National Extension College 1990.

Spelling

Self Access Spelling, Jan Hulley. Photocopiable. National Extension College 1991. Basic skills.

Spelling It Out, Rhiannedd Pratley, BBC 1988.

Spelling Made Easy, J.R. Evans, Macmillan 1985, EFL.

The Spelling Pack, ALBSU 1988.

Dictionaries

Longman Active Study Dictionary
Oxford Advanced Learner's Dictionary
Oxford Students Dictionary

English for study and vocational purposes

English for Business, Suzanne Looms, National Extension College, 1986.

English for Driving, Vivien Barr and Clare Fletcher, National Extension College, 1984.

Go to Work on Your English, a vocationally-based open learning series; National Extension College 1992.

Learning to Study in English, Brian Heaton and Don Dunmore, Macmillan 1992.

9 | Lesson Planning, Record Keeping and Evaluation

This chapter returns to the point left in Chapter 4 where an outline programme had been planned for a specified number of lessons. This chapter examines ways of planning an individual lesson, keeping records and evaluating learning.

The length of the lesson may vary but in adult education sessions are often two hours with a break, or one and a half without a break, so you can plan on one and a half hours teaching.

Planning a lesson

1. Deciding on your aims and objectives

You have virtually done this in your outline plan. There can be a range of teaching items in a lesson. You can aim to teach or practise:

- a particular language skill, e.g. listening
- to teach new vocabulary, e.g. computer, wordprocessor, keyboard, floppy disk, monitor.
- a grammatical item, e.g. the use of *some* and *any*
- a function, e.g. making comparisons.

You can revise/introduce/teach/practise/develop/or assess language. Aims can be described in terms of objectives: 'to practise listening to and writing down a message', or in terms of outcomes: 'The student will be able to listen to and write down a message'.

Remember that language learning is accumulative and you need to build on a student's existing skills. Constant practice and revision is also necessary for the language learnt to be retained.

In deciding on your aims consider:

- what a student already knows.
- how this lesson links with the previous lesson and fits in to the overall plan.
- whether there is a sensible ratio of new items to known items – not more than 20% new (although the first few lessons with a beginner will have to contain a higher proportion). This is a general rule but you may not know exactly what is new as you are constantly discovering what a student knows.

- whether the items may cause confusion if taught together, e.g. *in/on;* past simple *(I worked)*/present perfect *(I have worked).*

- how much you can reasonably do in the time allowed. This is something which is difficult to gauge at first but gets easier with experience and as you get to know a student.

2. Deciding on the content and methodology of the lesson

- consider how the language items are really used in English and in the selected contexts. Make sure your examples are accurate and natural.

- consider what language a student needs to understand either by listening or reading and what s/he needs to speak or write.

- decide what proportion of the time will be spent on the different skills.

- decide on the methods you are going to use to give the student practice in the language and skills.

- think about what you are going to do and what the student is going to do. Don't talk too much yourself. Provide plenty of opportunity for the student to repeat and practise.

- consider how you are going to demonstrate or explain the purpose of the activities and how to do them.

- consider whether there is enough variety in the lesson.

- consider whether there is development in the lesson, e.g. from controlled to freer practice.

- decide how much time you are going to spend on each activity.

- consider how you are going to check understanding and learning.

- decide on the materials (including visuals) you are going to use.

- decide on the equipment you will need, e.g. cassette recorder, video recorder.

3. Assessing and evaluating

As the lesson proceeds make a mental note of or jot down the things that cause difficulty and will need more work and the things that were done successfully. Identify any new learning needs that arise during the lesson.

At the end of the lesson allow a little more time to evaluate the lesson with the student:

- what was easy/difficult.

- what needs more practice.

- what was interesting/boring, etc.

LESSON PLAN

STUDENT			DATE	TIME
Sakeena				1 - 3pm

AIMS To teach some of the language needed for going to the doctor

OUTCOMES/ OBJECTIVES The student will have: revised names of parts of body, learnt vocabulary for symptoms, practised describing symptoms and answering doctor's questions, signing a prescription form

TIME	CONTENT	METHOD/ SKILLS	TUTOR	STUDENT	MATERIALS/ EQUIPMENT
1:00	Informal	Social chat			
1:05 Recap	Parts of body	Question/Answer L/S	Ask questions: What this? What are these?	Answer: It's (a) — they're my	Selves and/ or picture
1:10 Presentation	Symptoms: structure. I've got (a) - I feel ___ (+ He/She) Vocabulary	Presentation (student may know some words already) L/S	Describes symptoms	Listens e looks at pictures	Hand out - pictures to show symptoms
1:20 Practice Checking learning	What's the matter? + above Pronunciation	Drill L/S	Asks e answers ↓ Asks	Repeats Answers	"
1:40 Development 2:00 Tea break	Doctors questions Where? How long?	Dialogue L/S	Play cassette as often as necessary. Ask Q's to check understanding	Listen Answer Q's Repeat patient's part	Cassette recorder and tape
2:15 Check learning		Simple LSR role-play	Plays part of doctor	Plays patient	Cue Cards
2:35 Change of activity/ conclusion	Relevant sections of prescription form	Guided reading + writing L/S/R/W	Show and explain section about Children being exempt	Tick box. Find words 'Signed' 'date' NAME ADDRESS sign and date form	Copy of form
2:50 Evaluation	Asking and giving opinion	Discussion L/S/W	Ask questions Fill in record sheet	Give opinion	Record sheet.

TUTOR'S COMMENTS	(Evaluation and further learning needs). L = Listening R = Reading S = Speaking W = Writing

After the lesson jot down how you felt about it. Were the aims achieved? What went well/badly? Was the level all right? Was the student interested and motivated? Was progress made? What could have been done to improve the lesson?

4. Some other points to remember

- Correct what is important without over-correcting.
- Adjust your pace to what is necessary for a student. Move faster when the material is familiar, slower when it is new. If a student finds something easy, move on quickly, if difficult, slow up and go over it again and give more practice.
- Don't feel you have to stick exactly to your lesson plan.
- Be flexible. If a student comes along with something s/he needs to do straightaway, have an impromptu lesson and leave your planned lesson for another time. An example might be a letter the student has received, does not understand, and has to reply to. Make sure, however, that you do not just do the task for her/him. Make it into a teaching situation.

There is an example of a lesson plan on page 86.

Keeping a record

Although you will have your lesson plans and the student will have a file of work it is useful to keep a record sheet which summarises the work done in each lesson and which has space for student and tutor comments. These can take the form of ongoing assessment and evaluation. Items which need more practice and those which have been satisfactorily carried out can be noted and new learning needs recorded. The record sheet can be filled in by a student and/or yourself. You will be able to see at a glance what has been done.

Reviewing progress

It is important to review progress at regular intervals. This may be after a certain number of hours tuition, for example 20 hours, or half-way through and at the end of a short course.

Reviewing helps a student and tutor to see that progress has been made. Any difficulties a student has with the learning programme can be cleared up. You can plan the next stage of learning or decide on future action.

1. How to review progress

There are a number of ways of reviewing and assessing progress. You would need to choose one that is appropriate for a student and her/his purpose in learning English.

Here are some suggestions:

- observation by the tutor
- discussion between student and tutor
- checklist of language practised; student and tutor evaluate progress according to a scale, e.g. a little, quite a lot, a lot

PROGRESS REVIEW

Name .... **Date** ....

Tutor ....

GOAL To talk to the doctor and health visitor

SKILLS AND KNOWLEDGE	1	2	3	4
Parts of body	////	////	////	////
Describing symptoms	////	////	////	
Answering simple questions	////	////	////	

Evidence: How do I know I can do it?

Recording of role-play.
I took my daughter to the doctor
and could tell her what the matter was.

FUTURE PLANS:
Listening to doctor's instructions
Understanding
Reading names of medicines, instructions on medicine
Talking to health visitor about children

KEY:
1 = I have made a start.
2 = I have made some progress but need some more practice
3 = I have made a lot of progress.
4 = I feel confident about this now

- list of competences – tick and date when accomplished
- tasks set for assessment
- tests.

2. Evidence

A student may feel that s/he is now more confident in using the language needed for a particular context and is able to carry out a task satisfactorily. However, it is not enough just to say so. There must be evidence of achievement. This may take several forms. It could be:

- samples of work in a student's file. These may clearly show progression. For this reason it is important that they are *dated*
- recordings of spoken language
- comments by other people on a student's usage of the language
- instances of a student using the language outside the classroom.

Look back to the checklist on page 17 for the competences a student could work towards that should be identified in assessment.

Accreditation

Some students may want to have their learning accredited by gaining a nationally recognised certificate. There are a number of possibilities and different ones will suit different students. You need to be familiar with the range of accreditation available to be able to help a student to select what is most appropriate for him/her.

1. ESOL

The Royal Society of Arts Examining Board offers the Profile Certificate in ESOL. This is based on continuous assessment over 100 hours of tuition. Students can enter for one or all of the four language skills and have to show competence in at least three profile objectives. There are three levels of achievement. However, students cannot enter singly. There has to be a minimum number of entries in a class.

Pitmans offer ESOL tests in listening, reading and writing at five levels. They are functional in approach and are flexible because there is no syllabus to follow and the students can enter when they are ready.

2. EFL

There is a wide range of EFL examinations offered by the Royal Society of Arts (RSA) and The University of Cambridge Local Examinations Syndicate (UCLES) from elementary to advanced.

3. Basic Skills

These certificates are not specifically for ESOL students.

City and Guilds: Communication Skills (Wordpower) 3793. This is a competence-based form of assessment in which a student builds up a portfolio of evidence of her/his skills. This style is consistent with the framework for National Vocational Qualifications (NVQ), which are used for education and training for adults. It is offered at four levels: Foundation, Levels 1, 2 and 3. It includes reading, writing and oral communication skills. Wordpower assesses communication skills in everyday life situations. To assist a student to achieve the competence you would need to assess his/her strengths and weaknesses in that situation, and devise an appropriate learning programme.

Associated Examining Board: Achievement Tests; levels 1,2 and 3. Reading and writing skills. Assessment by examination whenever a group of students is ready.

Basic Test in English; higher level than the Achievement Tests. Listening, reading and writing; employment oriented aimed at school leavers. By examination at set times of the year.

You need to consider the following points when assisting a student to select an appropriate form of accreditation:

- Does it address the students needs and aspirations?
- Can it be used to accredit language competences being developed in different contexts?
- Can it be used to accredit a student's existing competence in English?
- Can the student undertake it at any time of the year?
- Is it suitable for the student's learning situation, e.g. in a group, 1:1 basis with a tutor, flexible drop-in workshop, as part of another course of training.
- Does it provide a route to other qualifications?
- Will it be widely recognised? e.g. a certificate specially designed for EFL or ESOL may not have the same status as those designed for native speakers.

Further reading

Assessing Reading: Using cloze procedures to assess reading skills, Judy Vaughan, ALBSU 1989 (Basic Skills).

Basic Skills Assessment Pack, ALBSU 1992 (Basic Skills).

ESOL, Wordpower and Accreditation, Sally Crofts, ALBSU Newsletter No.44, Winter 1992.

Planning a Programme/Assessing Progress, Scottish Community Education Council (Basic Skills).

Progress Profile, ALBSU 1990 (Basic Skills).

10 | Resources

This chapter looks at selecting and adapting resources, writing worksheets and using equipment.

The range of materials

The references in previous chapters show that there is a considerable range of resources that can be used by ESOL tutors and students. These can be grouped as follows:

1. ESOL Specific Materials. These fall into several broad groups:

(a) Everyday coping skills – topic based concentrating on spoken language and aimed at beginner and elementary students. Many of these are written for specific groupings, such as students in the home and in Community Groups, or from a particular ethnic background, e.g. *At Home in Britain; Talkback; Lessons from the Vietnamese.*

(b) Reading schemes aimed at beginner readers in English, e.g. *Brudenell Readers, Coventry Readers* – mainly for particular ethnic groups.

(c) Intermediate Level: Topic-based, everyday English including work and job search. All language skills used. Not directed at any particular ethnic group e.g. *Speak for Yourself; Topics and Skills; Time after Time* (grammar based).

(d) Materials aimed at good speakers who want to improve their literacy skills and/or grammatical accuracy. Most of these materials are self-access to enable students to work more independently but with some tutor support. This trend to self-access has increased with the growth of open-learning centres and flexible learning and distance learning approaches, e.g. *Self Access Worksheets; Self Access Grammar; Help Yourself to English* (National Extension College).

(e) Materials for language support in work, college and training situations. Again these materials usually need to be self access because students have to be able to work on their own with minimal teacher support. This is especially true when small numbers of ESOL students are involved, e.g. *English for Business; English for Driving; Go to work on your English* (National Extension College).

91

2. EFL materials

(a) General English – course books at all levels, skills practice, readers, games, communicative and pair work activities.

(b) English for Specific Purposes, e.g. business, catering, medical, study skills.

3. Adult literacy and basic skills materials

Reading, writing, numeracy and some oracy from beginner to pre-GCSE level.

4. Bi-lingual materials.

Some of the materials described above are bi-lingual, or partially bi-lingual, in that instructions and important vocabulary are given in English and some selected local community languages. Using bi-lingual materials gives value to a student's language and previous learning. It can make understanding easier and enable a student to work independently. Discuss with a student whether s/he wants to use such materials. S/he may not think it is necessary and some students may find it patronising.

5. Authentic materials

The real thing, not specially designed for teaching purposes.

Selecting materials

When you are looking at materials to choose something for a student it is useful to have a number of criteria in mind. This checklist will help you:

- Is it appropriate for use with adults?
- Does it take into account a learner's previously acquired skills and knowledge? e.g. a student's mother tongue.
- What does a student already have to be able to do to use the materials? e.g. know certain tenses, vocabulary.
- Are the contexts and examples relevant to the needs of an ESOL student?
- Does it lead to self-assessment and the development of learning skills?
- Is the level of language and the style suitable for an ESOL student?
- How long is it and how much work is covered?
- Is there a focus on the practical use of language?
- Is there any bias or stereotyping, cultural, sexist or racist?
- Is the presentation and layout clear and attractive? – size of print, legibility, amount on a page, illustrations.
- Do illustrations show people from different ethnic backgrounds?
- Are there any cultural references which might cause difficulty to an ESOL student?

- Is it interesting?
- Is it only for use with a class or can it be used with individuals?
- Can it be used by a student working independently?
- Can it be adapted to suit a particular learner?

If you think that a piece of material would be useful for a student but does not meet all the necessary requirements then you may be able to adapt it.

Adapting materials

1. Some ideas

The suggestions below apply to both spoken and written materials. Some adaptations can be very easy to make.

- If there are just a few words or phrases that are inappropriate or offensive you can blank them out or omit them.
- Instructions can be changed to make them suitable for a one to one situation.
- Instructions can be added to make the exercise self-access. These could be in English, in the mother tongue or on tape.
- Pictures or drawings can be added.

Other adaptations are more time-consuming so you need to consider whether it is worth doing or whether it would be better to look for something else.

- If you are using a piece of authentic material you will have to produce your own exercises.
- If you like the idea of an activity but not the content you could produce your own version.
- If the text is too long you can select from it or summarise it.
- If the text is too difficult (a) gloss or explain difficult words and phrases in simple English or in a student's mother tongue, (b) simplify the text.
- If the material is suitable but the activities based on it are not, then you can adapt them. For example, a recording may be at the right level for a student with good understanding but the activity may involve reading or writing which s/he is not able to do. You could help the student by devising activities within the student's competence.

Example

On the tape there is an announcement about a missing child. The instruction is simply: 'What does he look like? Listen to the tape and take notes.'

(a) You could draw three sketches of the child, two of them differing in essential details.

(b) Draw up a chart with multiple choice answers to be ticked:

Age	9 ☐	7 ☐	11 ☐
Coat	Blue ☐	Brown ☐	Black ☐

(c) Use a similar chart but the student fills in the information.

(d) Ask the student to make notes in the first language.

2. Simplifying a text

Assessing the difficulty of a text

There are formulae for measuring the difficulty of texts by looking at sentence length and word length, e.g. the Fogg Index. The level of difficulty is then described in a child-referenced reading age. This kind of measurement is inappropriate for judging adult reading material. The student's previous experience and present motivation are more important factors in assessing a text. It is quite adequate for you to analyse the text in terms of your knowledge of an individual student.

You have chosen a text because it is relevant for a student's needs, therefore the student should be well motivated to tackle it. You have assessed its general suitability in terms of the criteria described above.

You now need to consider:

- length of text – a very long text can be off-putting.
- length and complexity of sentences – the meaning can become lost in sub-clauses.
- length of words – a large number of words of three syllables or more adds to the difficulty of a text but it may be important to teach these words rather than paraphrase.
- repetition – the more repetition the easier the text.
- style – a straightforward, simple style is easier than an elaborate, flowery style.
- vocabulary – if there is a lot of unknown vocabulary but the words are important for student, you would be better to introduce these words gradually using simpler texts.
- grammatical structure – does it use tenses and constructions unfamiliar to the student? e.g. conditionals.
- print and layout – how can you improve or add to the text to make it easier to read? e.g. larger print, better spacing, line breaking, illustrations.

94

Stages of simplifying a text

- If you want to shorten the text select the main points. Do not omit anything that is important for overall meaning.

- Simplify vocabulary where appropriate. Do not remove essential technical words or familiar vocabulary merely because of their length. Omit idioms or colloquialisms.

- Break long sentences into shorter sentences. Keep to the most commonly used tense forms. Change passive forms to active forms, e.g. *'The bank was robbed by a masked gunman'*, becomes *'A masked gunman robbed the bank'*.

- Reduce the range of vocabulary by repeating words where appropriate.

- Add illustrations, maps or diagrams which will give clues to the meaning of the text.

- Write clearly and space the text well. Line break if this will be helpful.

Here is an example:

(i) An extract from 'The Food Hygiene Handbook' (necessary for food handlers).

Bacteria are microscopic organisms, often referred to as germs, which are found everywhere, including on and in man, on food, in water, soil and air.

Most bacteria are harmless and some are essential, for example, for breaking down decaying matter, or in cheese and yogurt manufacture. However, a small number of bacteria cause food spoilage and some, known as pathogens, are responsible for causing illness.

The number of bacteria present in food may be used to determine whether or not the food has been handled correctly.

A possible simplification.

Bacteria are very small living things. You can only see them with a microscope. They are often called germs.

Bacteria are everywhere. They are on and in people. They are on food, in water, soil and air.

Most bacteria do no harm and some bacteria are very important. For example, bacteria are necessary to make cheese and yogurt.

However, some bacteria make food bad and some make people ill.

A lot of bacteria in the food means you may have done something wrong.

A small number of bacteria means you have handled the food correctly.

(The Food Hygiene Handbook, Richard A. Sprenger, Highfield Publications)

Making your own worksheets

1. Points to consider

- When you make worksheets for a student make sure you are clear about the purpose of the worksheet. Is it to introduce a new skill or topic? Is it for revision or practice? Is it for information?
- What exactly is the language skill, function or grammatical structure you want a student to practise?
- What skills or knowledge does a student need to have to do the worksheet?
- Check the language of instruction. Sometimes the instructions can be more difficult than the language the student is to practise. It may be appropriate to use the mother tongue for the instructions or to put them on to tape. It is useful to teach a student the language of instruction and to some extent of grammatical terminology. Use standardised instructions to make it easier.
- Give examples to demonstrate what to do.
- Don't try to cover too much on each worksheet. It is better to have a series for a student to work through.
- Make sure the layout is clear. Use different sized letters, use upper case and lower case, underline and box items.
- Consider whether student will do the worksheet under your supervision or whether a student will do it on her/his own. If it is for independent work then it is very important the instructions are easy to understand. You may want to provide answers as well.

2. Layout

Worksheets should have the following elements;

- A title which shows the topic and the skill, function, language items practised. These can be related to an accreditation scheme if appropriate.
- The level – beginner, elementary, intermediate, advanced; or Foundation, Level 1, etc., if related to a scheme like Wordpower.
- Instructions clearly differentiated from the exercises.
- If the worksheet is part of a series it should also have a number.
- It may also be helpful to show what a student should already know, e.g. the past simple tense, and what might be needed to carry out the task, e.g. a dictionary.
- You may also want to provide an answer key.
- If there are other related worksheets refer the student to them.
- If other people may use your worksheets put your name on it so it can be attributed.

Using equipment

1. Cassette recorder

This is an indispensable aid for a language teacher. A number of ways of using a cassette recorder have already been mentioned.

To summarise:

- for listening comprehension either using published material or making your own recordings;
- for analysing a student's use of language;
- for discriminating elements of pronunciation;
- to allow a student to listen to her/himself and compare the pronunciation with a model;
- to record dialogues for a student to listen to and practise;
- to record a reading text to facilitate reading;
- to record instructions for worksheets.

When you make your own recordings it is best to use an external microphone to avoid buzz. If it is unidirectional you will not pick up surrounding noises.

When you are using the tape it helps to have a rev. counter so you can rewind and fast forward to the exact point you want.

2. Video

It may not be feasible to make your own videos but if you have access to a video recorder you can make good use of recordings of educational television programmes as well as commercially produced videos. The added dimension of vision as well as sound helps a student's comprehension. You can turn the sound down and see if the student can guess from the body language what people's attitudes are and what they might be saying.

3. Computers

The opportunity to develop computer skills in, for example, an open learning centre may attract some students who might not otherwise come for language tuition. Becoming computer literate is often a chance to improve employment prospects.

Language skills can be improved within this context. Whether a student wants to learn basic computer skills or work on vocationally linked programs there is plenty of scope for developing language support work.

There are educational programs aimed at the EFL and Adult Basic Skills market some of which may be suitable for ESOL students. Remember to apply the same criteria to computer programs as to any other resource. Use a student's first language where possible for instructions and information.

Some students find word processing very helpful when working on writing skills. If they have difficulty with the mechanics of handwriting the word processor frees them to concentrate on what they want to say and the finished result looks very professional. They can try out words and phrases, correct, move sentences and paragraphs about until they are satisfied with what they have written and how it is presented. They can use a spell check program if they are uncertain about spelling. Some wordprocessing programs can produce community languages so you could make bi-lingual materials and compare English structure with a student's mother tongue. A student could also develop writing in the community language.

The use of a concept keyboard gives many possibilities to create language programs for a student. This is an A4 or A3 electronic pad connected to the computer. It is divided into squares and when you press a square a word comes up on the screen. You can make overlays with pictures or words on to place on the concept keyboard and program the computer to display a matching word or sentence when the appropriate square is pressed. (From 'Using Computers with Bi-lingual students' see Further reading).

If you want to become aware of the published material available these catalogues will help you:

- *ALBSU Publications Catalogue.*
- *AVANTI Books Resources Guide;* 8 Parsons Green, Boulton Road, Stevenage, Herts SG1 4QG.
- *ESOL Materials Database;* Helen Sunderland, Language and Literacy Unit, Southwark College, London SE15 2RJ.
- *ESOL Materials Guide;* Training Agency.
- *NATECLA Resources Catalogue.*
- *The National Extension College Catalogue;* 18 Brooklands Avenue, Cambridge CB2 2HN.
- *Resources: A Guide to Basic Skills Materials;* ALBSU.
- *Basic Skills Software Guide;* ALBSU.
- *English for Speakers of Other Languages, Materials Guide;* TEED.

Language Development Network. This is a network of language support tutors in further education colleges which has been set up to pool and exchange language support and communication skills materials covering a range of academic and vocational contexts. Member colleges pay a fee and have to contribute materials on a termly basis. The colleges then have access to materials in the database. The materials are not available to non-members. The Language Development Network, Shipley College, Exhibition Road, Shipley, West Yorks.

Further reading

1000 Pictures for Teachers to Copy, Andrew Wright, Collins/Nelson 1984.

Making Materials, R. Leach, National Extension College 1985.

Using Computers with Bi-lingual Students, Glenys Smith, ALBSU Newsletter, No.45, Spring 1992.

ESOL books for teachers

Current Issues in Teaching English as a Second Language, S. Nicholls and E. Hoadley-Maidment, Nelson 1988.

Language Issues, produced twice a year: NATECLA (The National Association for English and Other Community Languages to Adults) – Hall Green College, 520-524 Stratford Road, Birmingham B11 4AI. NATECLA also produces a regular newsletter which has useful teaching tips and samples of material.

Glossary

Accreditation – recognising a person's skills by a qualification.

Active (of verbs) – the form of the verb when the subject does the action, e.g. Jim *cooked the dinner*.

Adjective – a word that describes the person or thing referred to by a noun – a *good* book; it's *interesting*.

Adverb – a word that tells you about a verb, e.g. She speaks *quickly*.

Articles – *a(n)*, *the*.

Authentic – language which is not specially composed for teaching – real language.

Bi-lingual – speaking and using two languages.

Cloze – a method of checking comprehension by omitting every 7th to 10th word and asking a student to fill in the gaps, using context and knowledge of structure.

Communicative – an approach to teaching which concentrates on the purposes of using language, i.e. functions.

Competence – a description of a skill or task to measure what a person can do.

Conditional clause – part of a sentence beginning with 'if' or 'unless'.

Consonant cluster – a group of consonant sounds, e.g. str, thr.

Consonants – all the letters of the alphabets except 'a,e,i,o,u'.

Content words – words that have a lot of meaning in themselves, e.g. book, pen, write, clever (i.e. nouns, verbs, adjectives).

Context – the situation in which language is used. The words/sentences that come before and after a word which help to give meaning.

Contraction – when two words are spoken as one – e.g. I will = I'll.

Cursive – joined up writing.

Decoding – working out how to read a word.

Dialogue – a scripted conversation for teaching purposes.

Diphthongs – a sound made up of two vowel sounds, e.g. 'oi' as in 'boy'.

Drill – practising sentences which follow the same pattern.

Functional – language described according to its purpose.

Gist – the main points.

Grammar – the rules for forming words and putting them together into sentences.

Grammatical feature item– a particular rule of grammar.

Information transfer – taking information from one source and representing it in a different way, e.g. from a text to a diagram.

Intonation – the way the voice goes up and down when speaking.

Key words – the 100 most commonly used words. The most important words to listen or look out for.

Language Functions – The purposes for which language is used, e.g. describing, explaining.

Line breaking – writing a sentence so that each word group is on a separate line.

Minimal pairs – two words that sound the same except for one sound, e.g. pen/pan.

Mono-lingual – speaking one language; a class of students who all speak the same language.

Monologue – when one person speaks without interruption.

Multi-lingual – speaking many languages, a class with students who speak different languages.

Noun – a word which names an object, place, person, feeling, e.g. book, Manchester, Jane, happiness.

Objectives – what you plan to achieve in a lesson, at the end of a learning programme.

Outcomes – what you actually do achieve in a lesson or a learning programme.

Passive (of verbs) – the form of the verb when the action is done to the subject, e.g. *The dinner is cooked.*

Performance criteria – the standards by which a task is assessed.

Phonetic – spelling which corresponds closely to sounds.

Prefix – a syllable added to the beginning of a word to change its meaning, e.g. happy/ *un*happy.

Preposition – words which show a relationship like time and place and are followed by a noun, pronoun, or the '–ing' form of the verb, e.g. *on* the table, *at* the weekend, *by* working hard.

Prior learning – skills that someone already has.

Productive skills – speaking and writing.

Pronoun – a word that is used instead of a noun, e.g. he, she, it.

Receptive skills – listening and reading.

Rhythm – the beat of the language.

Scan – to look quickly through a text to find a particular bit of information.

Self-access – being able to select materials and carry out learning activities independently with little help from a teacher.

Sentence patterns – sentences grouped together which have the same structure – There is/a picture/on the wall. There is/a book/on/the table.

Skim – to read quickly to get the main points.

Social sight words – words commonly seen in the street, etc, on signs and notices.

Stress – the emphasis put on part of a word, or a word in a sentence, e.g. *sen*tence; I *saw* him.

Structural words – a small number of frequently used words that give the framework to a sentence, e.g. The, a, this, to, some.

Structure – the way language is put together.

Study skills – essay writing, note-taking, using a dictionary, taking part in a discussion.

Substitution table – a chart of sentences which follow the same pattern for reading and writing practice.

Suffix – a syllable added to the end of a word, e.g. care/care*ful*.

Syllable – parts of a word which form a sound group, usually vowel plus consonant/consonant plus vowel, e.g. con/son/ant.

Tense – a form of a verb to show the time of an action, e.g. the present tense – I work.

Transferable skills – skills learnt in one situation/language which can be used in another.

Verb – a word describing an action or state. Every sentence has a verb, e.g. I *wrote* a letter, He *feels* happy, She *gets up* early.

Vowels – the letters 'a,e,i,o,u' – all words have a vowel.

Appendix

Further training opportunities for tutors

The City and Guilds Initial Certificate in Teaching Basic Skills (ESOL 9284) is an introduction to the teaching of ESOL. If you are interested in gaining a further qualification the following is available.

City and Guilds Certificate in Teaching Basic Skills (ESOL option) 9285. This is for practising teachers. It is a competence-based modular scheme, not a taught course. Prior learning and qualifications can be accredited.

Royal Society of Arts:

Initial Certificate in the Teaching of English as a Second Language to Adults. For volunteers and teachers with no ESOL training. Course lasts a minimum of 100 hours over 10 or 12 weeks.

Diploma in the Teaching of English as a Second Language in Further, Adult and Community Education. For practising teachers of ESOL. A course of a minimum of 100 hours usually over one year.

Index